Penguin Handbooks
Barbecues

James F. Marks was born in London in the early 1930s,
receiving his education in both England and Scotland. He
completed his national service with the Royal Engineers,
before embarking on a selling and marketing career which
covered products ranging from Bailey bridges to waste
disposal units. He subsequently formed Garden Appliances
Ltd, which has since become a major distributor in the
United Kingdom market of garden and leisure products.

He says that he has had 'a long-term interest in cookery
since discovering the joys – during my days as a wartime
evacuee – of bread dipped in a dried-egg mixture and fried
to a golden brown'. His interest in barbecuing stems from
his company's involvement in the sale of barbecues and
barbecue accessories, and this book is a result of his
experience in this field. He was instrumental in helping to
form SKEWER, a trade association, to educate the general
public in the joys and simple techniques of barbecuing.
This has led to his participation in radio and television
broadcasts on the subject.

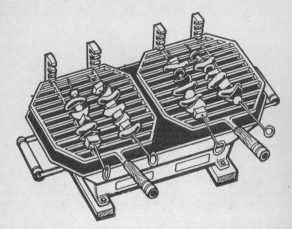

James F. Marks # Barbecues

Illustrated by Tony Odell

Penguin Books

Penguin Books Ltd, Harmondsworth,
Middlesex, England
Penguin Books, 625 Madison Avenue,
New York, New York 10022, U.S.A.
Penguin Books Australia Ltd, Ringwood,
Victoria, Australia
Penguin Books Canada Ltd, 2801 John Street,
Markham, Ontario, Canada L3R 1B4
Penguin Books (N.Z.) Ltd, 182–190 Wairau Road,
Auckland 10, New Zealand

First published 1977
Reprinted 1978
Copyright © James F. Marks, 1977
All rights reserved

Made and printed in Great Britain by
Hazell Watson & Viney Ltd, Aylesbury, Bucks
Set in Monotype Bembo

For Brenda, William, Helen and Duncan

Contents

2. *Attachments*

3. *Accessories*

4. *Fuel*

5. Fire lighters

6. The fire

7. Cooking

8. Buying meat for the barbecue

9. Basic instructions for barbecuing meat and fish

Introduction

Barbecuing is both an ancient art, and a relatively recent pastime.

Primitive man discovered, probably by accident, that meat tasted better roasted than raw, and he and his successors set about perfecting the means and the tools. Crude toasting forks of green twigs were replaced in the Iron Age by spits supported on fire dogs, and the wood fires of open camp sites eventually found their way to domestic hearth and kitchen range. The word barbecue itself, first used in the British colony of Virginia in the late seventeenth century, is supposed to denote spit roasting: a bastard form of 'de barbe à queue' (from beard to tail), adopted from French-speaking neighbours in Louisiana. As a word for an open-air social entertainment it was used in the United States in the early nineteenth century, the period of the great religious gatherings known as camp meetings. Later, and on a smaller scale, many families found that 'barbecuing' was fun and relatively inexpensive, making it possible to entertain friends, formally or informally, at a reasonable cost per head.

In the fifties and sixties of our own time, opposing forces worked mysteriously together to produce a real upsurge of interest: the affluence of suburban living, the trend away from urban suffocation in a 'return to the land' (be this the back garden) movement, and the machinations of a consumer society eager to switch from armaments to the hibachi (the plough being of little commercial interest these days). So, today, millions of people all over the world enjoy the delights of barbecued food.

This book contains all the practical advice you need to join them: a discussion of the various types of barbecue available, details of their accessories, hints on how to operate them to best advantage, and a wide selection of recipes.

Good cooking, and happy parties!

1　Barbecues

Basic considerations

Barbecuing is becoming increasingly popular in this country, both for informal cooking and for large-scale entertainment. The range of barbecues now available is wide and it is advisable to think carefully about the type and size that will be best suited to your needs. It is also helpful to look at various fully assembled barbecues, rather than make your choice from glossy sales literature alone. There are four basic questions which you should try to answer before buying a barbecue.

Outdoors or in?

Although one normally thinks of barbecuing as an outdoor activity, and most people will want a barbecue to use outdoors, it is possible to get units which can be used in the house. If you think the climate of your garden may not give you much opportunity to have cookouts you may want to consider a dual-purpose barbecue (p. 21) or one built into the fireplace. Ventilation is the crucial problem indoors, since charcoal gives off carbon monoxide fumes, but gas-fired or electric barbecues are free of this particular problem.

Open or covered?

A barbecue with a cover offers several advantages:

(a) Flare-ups, caused by grease dripping on the hot charcoal and igniting the oxygen at charcoal level, are eliminated. When the cover is closed, air enters through the vents in the bottom of the unit and is immediately consumed by the coals, thus allowing the heat to rise, reflect off the cover and cook the food as if in an oven.

(b) Heat is controlled by opening and closing the lower vents to allow more oxygen for greater heat and less for slower cooking. The top vent (in the cover) should always be open whilst cooking. An even temperature can be maintained on minimum fuel.

(c) Covered barbecues are able to perform efficiently in windy or wet conditions. The deeper their fire-bed and the more effective their dampers or air-vents, the better the temperature can be controlled.

(d) A covered barbecue can be used for smoke cooking (pp. 23, 25).

(e) Large roasts, turkeys, ducks and cuts such as brisket of beef are particularly suitable for the controlled slow cooking you can obtain from a covered barbecue. Heat reflecting off the cover allows the food to be cooked evenly on all sides, with relatively little attention. It should not be necessary to turn the food.

(f) Other foods can be cooked whilst meat is roasting, e.g. potatoes can be baked and foil-wrapped vegetables can be cooked. Some hooded barbecues have a warming oven with a separate door in the upper part of the hood.

The cover can either be an integral part of the barbecue or it can be an improvised accessory (p. 32).

Portable or permanent?

If you think you will use your barbecue regularly, and your garden or patio affords the space for it, you might consider a permanent fixture rather than a portable unit, whatever size of barbecue you need. Small ones are very easy to make yourself (p. 26) and larger ones have the advantage that working surfaces and storage spaces can be built in as required, as can warming ovens and other extras.

Buy or build?

For the more enterprising do-it-yourselfer building a fair-sized barbecue with or without all manner of useful accessories can be a stimulating challenge, but even the most ham-fisted cook could manage a small improvised unit. In fact, it may often be useful to experiment with such improvised barbecues in order to find the ideal location for more advanced ones, be they portable or permanent. Basic instructions for various types are given on pp. 19–20.

General requirements

Whatever type of barbecue you buy, its construction is extremely important. Grills should be made from nickel and chrome-plated steel, with the bars close enough together to prevent small sausages falling through. Spits and spit forks should also be heavy chrome-plated steel and if you intend cooking two or three chickens simultaneously, or perhaps a turkey or ham, check that the spit is sturdy enough to support the weight without bending unduly.

Above all, a barbecue must be stable, so check that it does not wobble unduly. Before buying a portable unit assure yourself, as far as possible, that screw-in or telescopic legs will stay put when the barbecue is erected *and* fully laden with charcoal and food.

Check the mechanism for raising and lowering the grill. The operating handle, preferably wood- or plastic-covered, should be located well away from the heat, and, bearing in mind that the grill will be raised or lowered when laden with food, the mechanism should move in an easy and positive manner.

The bowl and hood of some barbecues are made from porcelain-enamelled steel and this type of finish is excellent and long lasting though liable to chip and splinter unless the barbecue is handled carefully. Most barbecues, other than the cast-aluminium or cast-iron models, have a baked enamel finish and there should be no problem in keeping the fire-bowl in good condition providing the method of laying a fire described on p. 54 is followed.

When inspecting a heavy covered unit, check to see that the lid is reasonably close fitting. A hood should cover at least 50 per cent of the bowl. A lid that is fairly airtight when used

Simple improvised barbecue made from a large biscuit tin

in conjunction with an air-vent will allow accurate control of the temperature within the cooking area.

Improvised barbecues

Basically a barbecue is nothing more than a grill on which food can be cooked over a fire-bed of glowing coals. Very simple forms of this arrangement can be improvised with a grill-pan rack or double-thickness chicken wire on a large flowerpot, an old chrome-plated refrigerator rack on top of a large biscuit tin or over a frame of loose bricks, and so on. To make sure you have enough draught for the fire, raise the plant pot

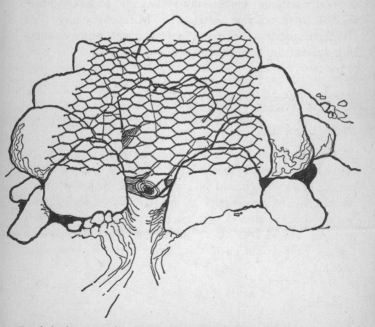

Beach barbecue with a piece of chicken wire spread over a ring of stones which surrounds the fire-bed

on bricks, punch holes in the biscuit tin or leave an air hole between the bricks.

The beach is an ideal place for a barbecue. You can of course take a picnic barbecue and a bag of fuel in your car or boat, but it is sometimes more fun to improvise. On a sandy beach make a hollow for the fire-bed and open up one or two channels into it from the side of the prevailing wind so that air can get to the fire. A ring of big stones (preferably dry) around the edge will help to support the temporary grill. On a pebbly beach build up a ring of largish stones to surround the fire-bed and again leave air holes. Collect driftwood for the fire and let it burn down to hot embers before embarking on cooking. Then all you need is a piece of chicken wire to act as a grill. This should be doubled over in order to reduce the hole size and give it extra rigidity. Metal coat-hangers can be adapted to serve as skewers. Even protective mittens can be improvised from heavy-duty foil.

Ready-made barbecues

Picnic barbecues

The size and design of picnic barbecues allows them to be easily stowed away in the car boot, or perhaps strapped to the outside of a rucksack, and this feature is their major attribute. Most picnic barbecues have 18-inch circular revolving grills but many different styles are available. Some models have a wind-shield and a few incorporate a small spit. An 18-inch circular grill should be adequate for a party of up to eight people.

Hibachi

This is a barbecue that originated in Japan but has proved to be very popular all over the world, especially to the newcomer to barbecuing, because of its basic simplicity and low cost. Round or rectangular hibachis are available in two styles – table-top or free-standing (on legs or pedestal) – and are usually manufactured from heavy cast black metal. Lightweight versions of the hibachi, made from pressed steel or aluminium in a variety of colours, are now available. The grill area on a hibachi is fairly small, perhaps capable of handling food for up to six people, although 'double' and 'triple' versions of the hibachi will be able to cope with larger quantities. Hibachis have draught controls in the side of the fire-bowl to assist the ignition of the charcoal and thereafter to control the rate of burning. Look for hibachis with a fire-bowl depth of at least three inches.

The ceramic *brasero* (of Mexican origin and very popular in the United States) is in essence the same thing.

Dual-purpose (inside/outside) barbecue

This is a barbecue designed to fit into the fireplace recess, thus allowing the smoke and fumes to be drawn up the chimney. The fire-pan and grill can be swung clear of the fireplace recess so that it is easy to handle food and fuel.

For outdoor use the barbecue is easily adapted by fitting a spike to it which can be driven into the ground.

Brazier barbecues

The next step up is the brazier (open) barbecue. Although very similar in many ways to the picnic barbecue the larger brazier models are more suitable for use in the garden or patio. The circular grill size of this particular style of barbecue ranges from 18 to 24 inches. Most models have folding or screw-in legs and the best versions have adjustable grills and wheels. A work-surface or small shelf can be most useful when cooking for several people on a high-standing barbecue and if one is not

Hibachi

Picnic

Brazier

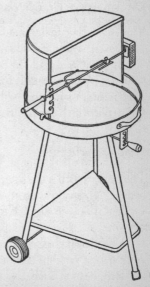

Hooded

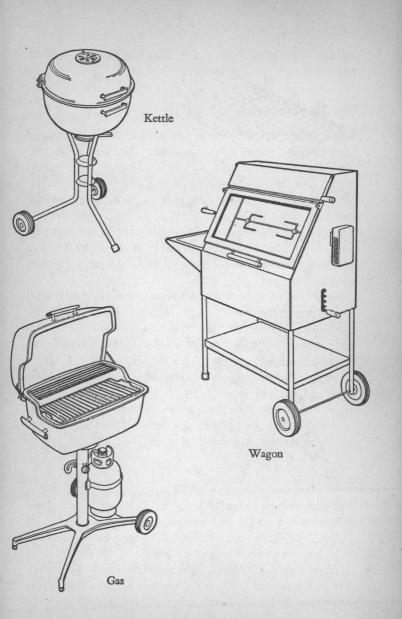

Kettle

Wagon

Gas

included with the brazier as a standard feature, it should be possible to purchase a clip-on tray.

Hooded barbecues

The basic difference between the hooded barbecue and the brazier barbecue is, of course, the hood. The hood fulfils two useful functions:

(a) To protect food cooking on the grill from the cooling effects of the breezes and help to prevent smoke swirling in the faces of the cook and guests.

(b) To provide support and mountings for a spit. Spits on these fairly large barbecues (usually 22–24 inch diameter grills) are normally rotated by an electric or battery operated motor.

Some hooded barbecues have a warming oven, usually with a door, inside the upper part of the hood. An oven is useful for keeping plates and cooked food warm and it means that larger quantities of food can be cooked in stages rather than in one long, hectic session. Other variations in the design of hooded barbecues include folding legs, detachable hoods, work shelves and wheels. The hooded barbecue is quite capable of catering for a party of twenty to twenty-five people provided that the bill of fare is not too ambitious (e.g. chicken pieces, hamburgers or something similar).

Kettle grills

The most effective covered barbecue is the kettle grill. Most versions are spherical or rectangular in shape, are generally made from either cast aluminium or porcelain enamelled steel and have wheels for easy moving.

The top half of the kettle grill is usually fixed to the lower half by hinges and when raised the top acts as a windbreak. When the lid is closed, the reflected heat within the dome browns the top of the meat in a way similar to that produced by oven cooking. The deep fire-bowl and the dome-shaped lid have adjustable vents to control the draught.

Should the cook find that the meat is cooking too quickly, the vents can be closed sufficiently to lower the level of heat. When cooking is completed, both vents can be fully closed to snuff out the live coals. Any charcoal left over can be used again. The kettle grill is considered ideal for barbecuing in exposed, windy locations and is excellent for smoking food. Spherical kettle grills are usually 18–22 inches in diameter.

For barbecue parties on a cool evening, the kettle's shape permits the guests to group around it, whilst the food is cooking, to take advantage of its radiant heat.

Wagon grills

The wagon grill, as the name denotes, is a large covered barbecue mounted on a wheeled wagon. The main body of the barbecue is usually of a rectangular-box shape but cylindrical versions are also available.

Wagon grills tend to be rather elaborate and sometimes include oven temperature gauges, warming ovens, heat-tempered glass panels in the door and built-in storage cabinets. These features are in keeping with a modern kitchen and, in some people's eyes, the similarity reduces the appeal barbecuing has as an impromptu, outdoor adventure.

Grill areas are large and the distance between food and coals can be adjusted either by raising the grill or lowering the fire pan (depending on the model). Most wagon grills have motorized spits. Some allow access to the fire by a separate door. Like the kettle grill the wagon grill allows efficient heat control, even on windy or wet days, and it can be used to smoke-cook meat or fish. Wagon grills are rather large and because of their size and weight, are confined to patio use. They are not particularly easy to dismantle and it is therefore wise to consider the problem of storage at the season's close before buying one.

Permanent structures

Building one's own barbecue can make good sense for those people who make barbecuing a regular habit. It is not only a way to save money (how much depends on the materials used) but it also provides the opportunity to create an attractive and useful garden feature. An added advantage is that when the barbecue is not being used as such, it can be used to burn garden or household rubbish.

The ideal time to undertake the design and construction of a barbecue is when the garden of a new house is being landscaped, or an existing garden is being re-designed. At this stage the barbecue can be easily situated in the best possible position and, in addition, can be constructed from materials being used for making walls and paths. Apart from economizing on building materials, the barbecue will blend well with its surroundings.

Unless you are a skilled bricklayer, or a proficient metal worker, keep your design simple and straightforward. The barbecue should be to scale with your garden and cooking requirements. The drawing illustrates a simple barbecue with a grill area large enough to cope comfortably with a party for twenty hungry adults.

It should not be much trouble to find suitable ironmongery for the barbecue at a local junk shop or scrap yard. The fire-pan and grill could be rescued from an old electric or gas cooker. Chrome-plated wire shelves from an old refrigerator also make useful and cheap grills. It is a good idea to buy two, or even three similar grills. Apart from having a spare grill to cover the possibility of one burning through, it will enable two grills to be placed at varying heights above the fire-pan and

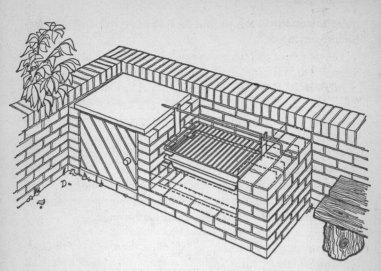

A permanent barbecue in your garden. By placing loose bricks in the front and side of the barbecue, as indicated by the dotted lines, it can be used to burn garden or household rubbish

thus allow better cooking control. Grills and pans come in different sizes and it is advisable to obtain these before proceeding any further with the design.

It is a good idea to line the inside of the barbecue with fire bricks, but this can prove fairly expensive. To save money try your local builders' merchant for broken fire-bricks, or a brickworks for over-burnt house bricks. Over-burnt bricks are able to withstand heat more successfully than 'soft' housing bricks (which are liable to crumble when subjected to high heat) or concrete building blocks (liable to crack open).

Siting your built-in barbecue is of great importance, as a mistake in location cannot be easily rectified. A spot should be selected, which, although sheltered from the direct onslaught of prevailing winds, is not in a completely protected position. If you are unsure where to locate the barbecue, experiment with improvised barbecues on a few loose bricks to see how quickly each fire builds up and the manner in which its smoke behaves.

The design of the barbecue can be as simple or elaborate as you wish to make it. Useful features worth considering include weatherproof fuel bins, warming ovens (mounted over, or adjacent to the barbecue), spit mountings and wind-shields.

If you decide to construct your barbecue away from the patio, it is advisable to pave the area immediately surrounding it. Paving can form an attractive feature, in addition to providing a stable surface for the cook to stand on. It is not a good idea to have grass growing right up to the base of the barbecue. Not only will it quickly become worn, but it may also become slippery and therefore hazardous in the late evening.

Storage

Storage is an important point to bear in mind when buying a barbecue. Some large units can be partially dismantled (hoods unclipped, legs folded away), but they, and even some of the small portable ones, are nevertheless bulky to store. Barbecues with a baked enamel finish should be stored under cover between use, or at least covered up with weather-proof sheeting. It is important to clean all barbecues thoroughly at the end of the season (use oven-cleaner on the metal grills, fire-pans, etc.) and to store them under cover.

Even in permanent structures the possibility of partial dismantling may be useful, as it will allow some of the more delicate metal parts (grill, spit mountings and such) to be stored under cover.

2 Attachments

Drip pan

A drip pan should always be used when cooking meat on a motor-driven spit. By placing the pan parallel to, and slightly forward of the spit rod, the juices and fat will be retained as they roll off the meat. The juice collected can either be used for basting purposes or may be blended into sauce or gravy. Correctly positioned, the drip pan will not only prevent juice from dropping on to the hot coals and producing excessive smoke, but will help to keep the fire base clean. By adding a small amount of water to the pan, the danger of the fat in the pan catching fire will be reduced.

Drip pans may also be used in indirect cooking, but then the pan should rest on the fire-base directly under the meat.

A drip pan can easily be made to fit any barbecue. Take an 18-inch roll of heavy-duty aluminium foil and tear off a strip about 3 inches longer than the pan you need. Fold foil in half lengthwise, shiny side out. Use a piece of wood or small book to help form the sides of the pan as shown in the sketch. Pulling the corners out and folding them back will provide leak-proof joints. The finished tray will be approximately 5 inches wide with $1-1\frac{1}{2}$ inch high sides. When using the pan for indirect cooking, make it as narrow as possible to minimize the reduction of reflected heat.

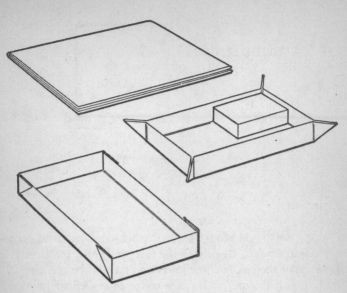

How to make a drip pan from aluminium foil

Elevating grate

Adjusting the distance between the food and the fire is one way of regulating temperature and cooking time. This can be done by means of a fire-tray fitted into a rack that can be raised or lowered by a crank mechanism. A number of the larger barbecues incorporate such a device in the frame that also carries the spit. It can also be bought separately to be built into a permanent brick barbecue.

Elevating grill

Serves the same purpose as the elevating grate and is of very similar construction. Instead of adjusting the heavy fire-tray you adjust the level of the grill. While sinking the grill into the heat-reflecting sides of the fire may have its advantages,

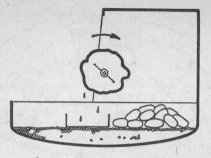

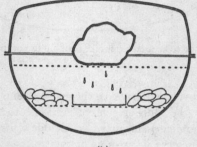

How to place a drip pan (*a*) when using a spit; (*b*) for grill cooking.
Make sure the drip pan does not rest on or against burning coals

many people will find it awkward to adjust to a varying
working level.

Hood or cover

Hoods act both as wind- and weather-shields and as a heat-
reflecting device which transforms your barbecue into an
effective oven. Half-hoods serve as little more than wind-
shields, but even this can be quite helpful when the unit has
wheels which enable it to be manoeuvred into the wind quite

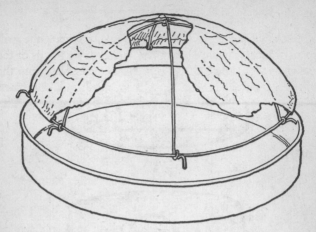

Improvised hood to be used for smoke cooking fish or meat on a brazier barbecue

easily. Full covers will have dampers or air-vents for temperature control (the more expensive versions often incorporate an air thermometer) and may also include separate compartments that can serve as warming drawers.

For people with an open brazier, who would like to try their hand at covered cooking, here is an easy method of making a cover from heavy-duty aluminium foil. Make a ring corresponding to the diameter of your brazier from 22-gauge galvanized steel wire. Bend three equal half hoops of wire and lash the hoops together, where they cross at the top, and where they touch the ring. The resulting frame should look rather like an upturned hanging flower basket. Cover the frame with strips of foil, dull side out, ensuring that the seams are folded tightly together. Remember that a really airtight cover would snuff out the flames! For occasional use an upside-down *wok*★ will do the trick.

★A Chinese frying pan with sloping sides; it looks rather like an upside-down coolie hat.

Hot-plate

The hot-plate, a slab of heavy cast metal, converts the grill into an outdoor stove. For toasting, and for frying eggs or the greasier cuts of meat (which would drip excessively into the fire) it is very useful indeed. Some barbecues have a combined grill and hot-plate, but loose plates can be fitted on most grills.

Kebab unit

An ingenious variation on the rotating spit consists of six or eight long skewers fitting a rack with a motor-drive belt which rotates the skewers by means of small toothed wheels fitted between blade and handle. One version of this unit can be secured directly to a standard spit.

Spit, spit motor, balance weights

The barbecue spit, like any other spit, is basically just a steel rod on which poultry or cuts of meat can be impaled. A fork attachment on one or both sides can be adjusted to hold the food in position. The spit rests on a cradle or simple supports sticking up on either side of the fire-box or mounted on the sides of the hood. It may be rotated by hand, in quarter turns on a locking device, but the motor-drive variety is more popular.

A very few barbecues allow the fire-pan to be placed vertically as well as horizontally. The increasing popularity of vertical spit roasts such as doner kebabs may create more demand for this type. Spit motors have a lot of heavy work to do – perhaps running for a period of several hours – but good-quality electric motors should be capable of turning 15–20 pounds of meat at about 4 r.p.m. If the barbecue of your choice is of American origin you can be assured of the motor's quality and performance by checking to see if the motor casing is stamped 'UL approved'.

To ensure easy movement it is essential that the spit be evenly loaded: irregular-shaped cuts may need balance weights to adjust their tendency to drag. Another necessary accessory is a pair of pliers for adjusting and tightening screws of the spit forks.

Tool rack

Some of the larger wagon grills incorporate tool racks, and when planning a permanent barbecue you should leave space for one. The long handled tools usually sold in standard kitchen racks are quite suitable for use with a barbecue.

Warming spaces

The hoods of some of the more elaborate barbecues have warming ovens built in, and with permanent structures it is easy to plan such spaces below or next to the fire-box. Small barbecues such as the hibachi can serve as secondary units to larger ones simply to keep food hot. For occasional use, a double-boiler with hot water in the lower part may do, and heated rock salt packed around one container inside a larger one will keep food quite hot for at least an hour.

Wind-shield

If your intended picnic site is going to be, more often than not, an open beach, the picnic barbecue selected should incorporate a wind-shield. In fact, wind-shields are only useful with the small barbecues: for larger models a hood is much to be preferred.

Work surface

Whatever barbecue you use, allow yourself plenty of working space as close to it as possible and at a convenient height (about three feet). Some units have flap tables attached; small portable barbecues can be put on top of a working table, picnic table, or even a trolley. Do not underestimate the danger of working at an inconvenient height, especially ground level.

3 Accessories

Accessories to the barbecue

Cleaning materials, brush, detergent, oven-cleaner

A metal brush to clean the grill and other metal parts to which food may stick. Oven-cleaner to clean the fire-pan and the rest of the barbecue at the end of the season. Detergent and hot water to wash the gravel if it gets very greasy. Removing the grill immediately after use and wrapping it in wet newspaper or paper towel will make it easy to clean after the meal.

Fire starters

See Chapter 5, p. 50.

Foil

Heavy-duty aluminium foil has numerous uses in barbecue cooking. It can be used, shiny side out, to line the fire-bowl and the hood, thus increasing its heat-effectiveness. Hoods and covers for pots can be fashioned from foil, as can basting cups and (as described on p. 29) drip pans. A double layer of foil on the grill makes a useful hot-plate: prick the foil with a fork for cooking hamburgers, but not for bacon. Fish or vegetables wrapped in a double thickness of foil will grill easily.

Fuel

See separate chapter, pp. 47–9.

Gloves and apron

Protective clothing is no exaggerated luxury when working a barbecue. Oven gloves or asbestos mittens are absolutely indispensable, and a good quality working apron is also no more than a minimum requirement.

Gravel

If the fire-bowl of your barbecue does not have perforations or air-vents you can improve its bottom draught by putting a layer of coarse gravel on the bottom. If the gravel needs cleaning it can be washed in hot water with detergent, but take care to dry it thoroughly before use or steam pressure in small cracks may cause stones to explode.

Lights

Should you contemplate using your barbecue in the late evening, perhaps for a dinner party alfresco, or a Guy Fawkes party, it is important to provide adequate lighting. For a permanent installation which needs underground cable from the house, or garage, to the lamp, it is advisable to have the work done by a qualified electrician. Excellent garden lighting kits are available from garden centres, department and hardware stores and these have the advantage of being relatively simple to set up on a do-it-yourself basis. A cheaper, but quite effective way of bringing light to the barbecue area, is to hang hurricane lamps in the surrounding trees or simply stand them nearby.

Tongs

Long-handled tongs are the best tool for coping with the fire while you are cooking. They make it possible to move individual coals either away from or into the fire without causing flare-ups, which are almost unavoidable if you use a poker.

Accessories for cooking

Baster

Spit cooking especially needs frequent basting. A tube baster is ideal, but a basting cup can also be improvised from tin foil. For basting other than on a spit, a brush is less likely to cause flare-ups.

Boards

Sturdy wooden boards for cutting and carving.

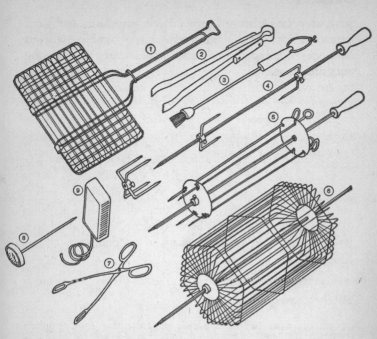

Barbecue accessories: 1. Hinged wire basket (broiler); 2. Long-handled tongs; 3. Long-handled basting brush; 4. Spit with adjustable tines; 5. Spit with shish-kebab attachment; 6. Spit basket; 7. Short tongs; 8. Meat thermometer; 9. Spit motor (electric or battery operated)

Brushes

Fat is more evenly applied to the food with a brush. It is useful to keep a second brush for applying sauces and seasoning. Brushes should be made of pure bristle; do not use brushes made from nylon or plastic.

Foil

The uses of foil are not limited to those already mentioned on p. 36. As in the kitchen, it is the ideal wrap for food that can be slow cooked in its own steam (lamb, vegetables, fruit) and for pit and coal cooking. Protruding bits of food like chicken wings or fish tails can be protected from burning and charring with a foil cover.

Foilware

The great range of foilware plates and dishes and divided serving plates make excellent barbecue-to-table cookware.

Forks

Like all tools used for barbecue cooking, forks should be long-handled, and preferably have a wooden grip, even a hand-guard.

Kitchen towel

A roll of paper towels is the easiest thing for mopping up, wrapping smelly garbage, or just wiping your hands.

Knives

Preparation of food for a barbecue needs at least the same array of sharp and strong carving, slicing and paring knives as you would use in the kitchen. If anything their quality should be rather higher, to overcome the hazards of working outdoors and often on less convenient working surfaces.

Pans

What pans you will need with your barbecue depends, of course, on what you intend to cook. As a general rule, choose very heavy cast metal saucepans, casseroles and frying pans and whatever their size see that they have long handles which do not become too hot too quickly.

Skewers

Choose long skewers with a good handle and preferably a hand-shield. If you do a lot of skewer cooking, a kebab unit (p. 33) may be useful.

Smoke chips

Smoke caused by fat dripping into the fire is not usually an improvement but the more aromatic smoke given off by some hardwoods (hickory) and most fruit woods does improve the flavour of barbecued food. If you can, use green sprigs on top of the fire (or soak dry wood thoroughly before use) but it is also possible to buy bags of 'smoke chips'. Fresh herbs on the fire quickly impart their flavour to the food and should not be used until the last few minutes of cooking.

Spoons

Again, long-handled and with a heat-resistant handle. Metal spoons become unbearably hot all too quickly and wooden ones are likely to get burned.

Sprinkler

To douse unwanted flames and flare-ups some sort of water sprinkler is a necessary aid. A water pistol may do, if it is not too powerful (water should be used sparingly or the whole fire may suffer), but the small sprays used for ironing or plants are perhaps the most convenient.

Strong string

Good twine will often be necessary for trussing birds and roasts of irregular shape.

Thermometers

Two very different types of thermometer are useful for barbecue cooking. Indispensable for all roasts and an asset in cooking fish is the meat thermometer; pushed into the centre of the food (taking care not to touch bone or spit) it will give you an accurate idea of the inside temperature which determines whether a roast is rare or well-done and whether fish is adequately cooked. Beware pockets of fat: these will give too low a reading. See the charts on pp. 62 and 66 for readings. An air thermometer is useful only in covered cooking, and some hooded barbecues have one as a standard feature.

Tongs

Long-handled tongs, similar to the ones you use for moving coals in the fire, are useful for moving foil-wrapped parcels or pieces of meat you do not want to pierce for fear of losing the cooking juices.

Waste bin

Adequate provision should be made not only for the garbage you create while cooking, but also to cope with paper napkins, plates and such after use.

Wire basket

A hinged wire basket, a variation of the type used to beat soap into the wash before the advent of detergents and powders, will hold fish, patties and other soft and easily-damaged food firmly together during the cooking. Another variation on this theme is the revolving grill, an arrangement of two grills used to sandwich food and clamp into the spit forks for mechanical turning. Special spit baskets made of wire are available, both flat (to prevent food from turning over) and cylindrical (to allow food like chicken pieces to tumble freely).

Accessories for serving

Bowls

Although it is customary for people to help themselves to the cooked food straight from the barbecue, you will need metal or wooden serving bowls for things like salads and sauces.

Bread basket

A basket is the easiest way to cope with rolls, toast or sliced bread.

Coffee-pot

Either a percolator which will make coffee right there on the fire, or a metal pot which will keep ready-made coffee hot by the side of the fire, or a thermos.

Cups

Breakage tends to be higher in the rough-and-ready surroundings of most barbecues, so plastic or plastic-coated paper cups are advisable for most drinks.

Cutlery

Cutlery can be kept to a minimum, as much of what is traditionally cooked at barbecue parties is finger food. Most plastic cutlery will do quite well and can be cleaned or thrown away as you like. Steak knives, however, should be sharp: what is the use of providing good (and expensive) meat if it is only killed all over again with an inadequate knife?

Foilware

See note on p. 40.

Ice bucket

As necessary as a good coffee-pot, and for a similar reason: if the wine or the lemonade have the same temperature as the coffee the party spirit will soon be lukewarm.

Openers

You will probably need both tin and bottle openers.

Paper napkins

A good supply of paper napkins is essential. The napkins should be strong but absorbent, and of a fair size. Squares of kitchen paper will do very well, but the small gaily-coloured flimsies which take neither grease nor water will not.

Pepper and salt

A good large pepper-mill and an equally sturdy salt-shaker are musts. You will probably also want a standard selection of sauce and dressing bottles, whether you make your own or buy them ready made.

Plates

Same observation as for cups. Paper plates will do for most occasions, or you can invest in a stack of unbreakable plastic ones.

Serving spoons

Apart from at least one salad set you may need serving spoons for sauces or vegetables. Use long-handled ones if you serve from barbecue-to-table pots.

Accessories in case of accidents

Bug-repellent spray

Both the food and the lights of your barbecue party will attract all sorts of insects. Lights set fairly high at a slight distance will keep the moths at bay, but for the others a spray may be the only answer. Avoid squirting over open food.

Burn lotion

A jar of some effective ointment or the old-fashioned remedy of linseed oil and lime-water should form part of your standard barbecue kit.

First-aid kit

Apart from bugs and burns, I fail to see why your barbecue party should be more accident-prone than any indoor gathering, but for picnics away from home it makes sense to carry a small kit (plasters, aspirin and an antiseptic are about the minimum).

4   Fuel

Most household barbecues use charcoal to fuel their fire, and a very few large ones can also use wood; wood is the standard fuel for pit cooking (pp. 68–9). An oddity is the special small barbecue which will cook a steak on no more than half a newspaper; electric and gas-fired barbecues are another special development.

Charcoal

Charcoal is generally available in two forms, as lumpwood charcoal or as uniformly pressed briquets. *

Charcoal briquets

Charcoal in briquet form is recommended to give the best results, from the cook's point of view. The briquets burn for a long time, with little smoke or odour, and produce a uniform intense heat without the nuisance – usually associated with high resin softwoods – of sparks popping up. Best-quality charcoal briquets are made from dense hardwoods with a low resin content, such as beech, oak and birch.

Charcoal briquets with a mineral content are considered to give off a slightly greater heat than do the pure hardwood briquets but they tend to be less popular with the barbecuer.

Mineral briquets are made from selected mineral carbons which are pulverized and then bound, with starch, into egg-size briquets.

Some brands of charcoal briquets are specially treated to ignite more easily. Briquets, unless specially treated with an ignition agent, require several minutes of intense heat to become ignited. When burning they simply glow instead of flaming, unless there is a considerable draught. In daylight you may not see the glow, just the fine grey ash that appears on the surface of each briquet as the fire spreads through it.

Lumpwood charcoal

Lumpwood charcoal is made from either softwood or hardwood but softwood is the most common. Lumpwood charcoal is made by the ancient method of charring wood in a kiln. Charcoal from the kiln comes in lumps of varying size and is easier to ignite than the briquet form. However, because the charcoal burner habitually uses a mixture of woods, lumpwood charcoal, also known as scrap-wood charcoal, has a tendency to give off sparks and, because of its high resin content, may give the food a slight flavour. It also burns up rather faster than the compact briquets.

Whether you prefer briquets or lumpwood charcoal, buy a good-quality, dependable brand. The success of your barbecue party may depend on the charcoal you use and it is almost certainly false economy to buy the cheapest. Should you have any difficulty in starting the fire, try another brand of fuel for your next barbecue session, and always store your fuel in a dry place.

Charcoal, when burning, gives off carbon monoxide gas. It is therefore highly dangerous to cook with it in a closed room unless the barbecue can be sited inside the fireplace recess, thus allowing the fumes to be safely drawn up the chimney.

Wood

For large barbecues and for pit cooking only hardwood should be used, or good-quality fruit woods. Softwoods are usually resinous and tend to flare and give off smoke which will not do the flavour of your food any good. Softwoods also burn too fast and do not leave much glowing coal.

Gas and electricity

For people who wish to enjoy some of the pleasures of barbecuing without getting involved in the preparation of a charcoal barbecue, gas and electricity provide the answer.

In both gas and electric barbecues, natural lava rock, or a similar man-made product, is used in lieu of charcoal: when heated by the gas flame or an electric element (like that of a kettle) the rock emits a radiant heat. The heat level is controlled, as for a kitchen oven, by the turn of a knob. After cooking is completed the greasy lava rock can be cleaned by placing a piece of aluminium foil loosely on top of the heating element and rock, and turning the control knob to its highest setting. After ten minutes or so, most of the grease and impurities in the rocks will have been burnt off.

Both gas and electric barbecues can be used to smoke food provided, of course, that they have a hood. This is done by placing a small quantity of dampened hickory or apple-wood chips onto the heated rock and then keeping the hood closed.

Some small electric units just heat a grill plate directly; their use is rather limited.

Most gas barbecues can be adapted for use with either natural or L.P. (liquid propane) bottled gas.

For indoor use these types have the advantage that their ventilation requirements are little more than those of an ordinary stove.

5 Fire Lighters

Self-igniting charcoal

Perhaps the simplest, but certainly not the cheapest or fastest, method of starting a fire is to buy a small pack of specially treated briquets (in some cases the pack itself is treated with an ignition agent). The pack is placed on the fire-bed and lit. The contents are in turn ignited and the coals should be ready in 30–40 minutes.

Chimney

Although a fire can be started with paper and kindling wood, this method is not recommended, as generally speaking it is both messy and inefficient, unless you go to the additional trouble of making a special fire-lighting chimney out of a tall tin. Open the tin at both ends, make air holes around the bottom end, fill it up with charcoal and light a kindling fire under the whole thing. Remove the chimney when the charcoal is ready for cooking.

Solid and granulated fire starters

The familiar solid white block fire starter has been available from hardware shops for many years and has always been popular as a cheap, safe and efficient domestic fire starter. Made from petroleum distillate and urea formaldehyde, the solid starter is usually available in an easily broken block. Break off two or three pieces and place them between the base and halfway up the side of the briquet pyramid. After lighting, the starter will burn for over fifteen minutes. The coals should be ready for cooking in 30–40 minutes.

The same solid white starter is now available in granulated form which provides a slightly faster ignition than the solid block. Build a pyramid of briquets and sprinkle the granules in the air spaces to allow a 'wicking' action. The granules can be safely lit with a match or taper at several points. This ensures a quick spread of fire and the coals should be ready for cooking in 20–30 minutes.

Liquid fire starter

Carefully follow the manufacturer's instructions. Arrange a pyramid of twenty to twenty-five briquets on the fire-bed of the brazier bowl or fire-box, then pour liquid on to the cold briquets. Close the container and wait for a minute or so for the liquid to soak in, then light the briquets (use a long match or taper). The fire is ready for cooking when most of the briquets are covered in grey ash (30–45 minutes).

Keeping a small supply of briquets that have soaked in a

container (a wide-mouthed jar will do) of liquid fire starter will help to speed up the fire starting process – just add two or three of these soaked briquets at the base of the pyramid, cover them up with the dry briquets and light.

Liquid fire starter is substantially the same as paint thinner which is usually cheaper.

Jellied alcohol or 'canned heat'

Arrange a pyramid of briquets directly on the fire-bed. Place two or three teaspoonfuls of the jelly well down into cavities near the base of the pile. Close and remove the jelly container before lighting the jelly. The coals should be ready for cooking in 30–45 minutes when a grey ash covers most of the briquets.

Electric fire starters

Portable electric fire starters provide a sure, fast and clean method of starting. The electric starter element (a simpler version of the kettle element) is placed near the base of the briquet pyramid and some 5–10 minutes after being switched on can be removed, as by then the briquets should be burning properly. Re-make the pile, using long-handled tongs, and 20–30 minutes after starting, the briquets should be ready for cooking. Some of the more expensive barbecues have a built-in electric fire starter.

Gas torch (blow-lamp)

Fast results can be achieved by using one of the compact gas pressure torches normally used for paint stripping, welding, etc. Arrange briquets one layer deep, but crowded together. Slowly pass the flame over the briquets until the fire is visibly started.

Another way of using gas to aid your fire-lighting is to ignite your charcoal on a strong metal frame (like a riddle) over the gas ring in your kitchen. It is a messy method, and mind the ventilation.

6   The Fire

A successful barbecue begins from a properly laid fire, and a little time taken in the preparation of the fire-base and the selected starting method will result in clean, economic and controlled cooking.

Preparing the fire-bed

Fire-bowls for most small units or the fire-pan on a wagon grill will not allow air to circulate up through the briquets if these are laid directly on the bottom. Lack of air under and passing through the briquets will result in the fire starting and spreading very slowly. This disadvantage can be overcome by use of a gravel or specially manufactured fire-base.

The first step is to line the fire-bowl of the unit (having removed grill and the pivot lift-pin), or the fire-pan of the wagon grill, with aluminium foil. Use enough heavy-duty foil to cover the entire bowl and keep the lining in position by tucking the edge over the bowl's rim. Keep the shiny side of the foil up to reflect the heat back towards the cooking area. Apart from reflecting the heat, the lining protects the bowl, makes cleaning easier and reduces fuel waste.

Pour in sufficient fire-base – vermiculite (obtainable from builders' merchants), or dry, clean gravel (approximately a quarter of an inch in diameter) – to cover the base of the bowl.

The material used should be evenly spread to a depth of approximately one and a half inches at the centre of the bowl. Wagon grill fire-pans should be evenly covered to a depth of

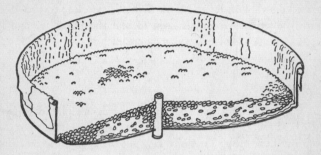

Section through a barbecue illustrating how the fire-bed should be laid

approximately one inch. This fire-base supports the briquets and allows air to pass under and through them so that they can 'breathe' and burn more evenly.

It is not necessary to change a properly prepared fire-bed after each cooking session. Depending on the amount of grease absorbed by porous base materials or coating the gravel, and the amount of ash clogging the fire-base (too much ash will prevent a draught from circulating under and between the briquets), the fire-bed could last all summer. However, it is advisable to discard the porous materials or wash the gravel after four to six barbecues. The gravel can be cleaned in a bucket of hot water and detergent. After rinsing well and *thoroughly drying* it can be used again on a new foil lining.

Some barbecues – the kettle grill is an example – are fitted with a fire-bed grid on which to lay the charcoal briquets. Apart from ensuring that the grid openings are not clogged, no fire-bed preparation is required as the air will circulate freely through the grid as the air above the fire is heated and rises.

Direct heat

When grilling those cuts of meat which require fast cooking, e.g. steaks, chicken pieces, chops, hamburgers, the fire-bed is located directly under the food. Direct heat close to the food (with the grill lowered) is used to seal the juices in, and if desired, create a charred, crusty exterior.

Reflected heat

For spit barbecuing and roasting the coals are placed so that their heat will be indirectly applied to the sides rather than the bottom of the meat. That is to say, put the coals either at front and rear with a drip pan in the middle or towards the back only with a drip pan catching the fat off the spit as it swings the meat forward and upward.

Wood fire

A good wood fire will need at least two hours to build, fire and burn down to usable coals. The wood fire needed for pit cooking takes a good deal longer, since it is not directly involved in the cooking process but only heats up what is, in effect, a giant Dutch oven.

The amount of fuel to use

Novice barbecue cooks tend to use far too much fuel. Apart from being an unnecessary waste, excess fuel often produces food which is heavily charred on the outside whilst somewhat raw inside. With practice one learns to use modest quantities but the following notes provide a guide on how to estimate the amount of fuel required.

Hibachi and brazier barbecues

The fire-bed should be made of enough briquets to cover it with gaps of about an inch between briquets to allow ventilation. For a 24-inch unit this will total approximately forty-five briquets, while an 18-inch model will need about twenty-five (the average five-pound bag contains roughly sixty briquets). This amount of fuel should be adequate for a burning time of one to one and a half hours and give sufficient heat to cook a full grill of chicken pieces, steak or similar food.

Kettle and wagon barbecues

These require less fuel than the open units – more details can be found on pp. 16 and 65.

Spit cooking

Most spit cooking, for example for a four-pound chicken or a similar piece of meat, will need only two full rows of briquets along the back of the bowl. For a 24-inch bowl this will be about twenty briquets, and for an 18-inch one fourteen. For larger pieces, add a second layer of briquets on top of the first. This should give you a cooking time of up to two and a half hours.

Lighting the fuel

To ignite the briquets and get them ready for building a fire-bed, use one of the methods described under 'Fire Lighters', pp. 50–53.

After building a fire by one of these methods it is possible to accelerate the coals' state of readiness by creating a draught. Hand-operated bellows and electric fans are excellent for this purpose. Opening the covers and vents of the kettle grills and wagon grills will create a positive draught but remember to keep a watchful eye on the fire's progress during this period to ensure against the creation of a miniature furnace, and do not use a forced draught after the meat is on the grill or spit, otherwise ash will be blown over the food and ruin it. A windy day will also speed up ignition time. The average time you will need for lighting the charcoal, arranging the fire-bed and getting the coals ready for cooking over will be about forty-five minutes. The coals are ready for use when all flames have died and a fine grey ash covers the surface entirely.

Controlling the heat

Once the charcoal has been properly lit and an adequate fire-bed prepared, the only problem that remains is that of heat control. This can be achieved by a variety of methods:

(a) By means of dampers or air-vents (covered barbecues): the greater the draught the fiercer the fire.

(b) Altering the distance between fire-bed and grill – see the note on elevating grates and grills on p. 30.

(c) Increasing or decreasing the distance between individual briquets: the closer together the briquets the more intense the resulting heat.

(d) Since barbecue cooking is done not by a direct fire but by the infra-red radiation given off by the coals, anything that shields this radiation slows the cooking process: it is usually advisable to tap off the excess ashes at regular intervals, but sometimes the ashes may serve to dampen a slightly too hot fire in due course.

For longer cooking times it is advisable to keep a reserve of briquets warming up around the edges of the active fire-bed: cold coals added to the bed will substantially diminish its effectiveness. Occasional flare-ups, whether in lumpwood charcoal or from dripping fat, are easily handled with a small water spray, applied as lightly and as locally as possible so as not to harm the main bed.

Snuffing the fire

When your cooking session is finished, snuff out the coals and store them for later use. In covered barbecues the snuffing is done simply by closing the dampers in top and bottom. From smaller units the coals can either be transferred to a coal bucket with a lid which, when closed, will fulfil the same function, or dunked into a bowl of water and afterwards left to dry out.

Never pour water over the barbecue itself to put out the coals: the sudden shock may warp or damage the metal.

7   Cooking

On the grill

Of the various barbecue methods open grill cooking is the
most popular. It is ideal for chicken pieces, chops, sausages,
hamburgers, small fish and other foods that can be cooked
fairly quickly. When barbecuing on an open grill, it must be
borne in mind that the speed of cooking is affected by wind
and air-temperature conditions. General advice on grilling
times is given in the table but after some experience your own
judgement should serve as a reliable guide. To avoid the
hazards of fat dripping into the fire it helps somewhat to tilt the
grill forward slightly, and to arrange the fire in such a way that
you can have a narrow drip pan in front of it. Meat should be
removed from the refrigerator or freezer in good time to
allow it to reach room temperature. Basting with prepared
sauces, especially those with a strong flavour, should preferably be carried out during the last few minutes of grilling
otherwise the sauce flavour may swamp the natural flavours.
On the other hand, bastes leave little taste anywhere but on the
surface, and a better effect is often achieved by marinating.

Grilling procedure

1. Start your fire by following the instructions contained in
Chapter 5. Wait until tops of briquets are covered with grey
ash. Knock the ash off before starting on the food.

2. Rub grill with a little fat or cooking oil to lubricate it. This will help to prevent the meat from sticking to the grill.

3. Place meat on the grill, adjusted to a position two to three inches above the coals. Cooking at this level for a minute or so will sear the meat and this helps to seal in and preserve some of the juices otherwise lost when barbecuing over an open grill. After searing the meat, raise the grill to about four inches.

On skewers

The simplest way of barbecue cooking, which must have pre-dated both grill and spit cooking, makes use of thin metal rods to secure anything that is to be cooked by simply piercing it. The rods can be arranged over the simplest camp-fire with the help of a few bricks or anything else that provides a firm edge to the fire. The smallest barbecue will cook skewered food, and at the other end of the scale is the sophistication of electrically rotated kebab units (see p. 33). Flare-ups from dripping fat are harder to avoid in skewer cooking than with any other method. If you have plenty of space you can arrange your coals in rows parallel to but not directly under the skewers.

On a spit

Spit cooking is really the only true form of roasting. It is an excellent and popular way to cook rib of beef, loin of pork, ham, leg of lamb, poultry and large fish. Most, if not all, hooded barbecues and wagon grills incorporate rotisserie equipment while separate attachments are available even for very small units. For practical purposes, the spit should be powered by an electric or battery-operated motor.

Grilling time-chart

Food Type	Cut	Size or Weight	Recommended Fire-heat	Approximate Cooking Time (each side) in minutes		
				rare	medium	well-done
Beef	steak	1 in.	hot	5–6	7–8	10–12
	steak*	1½ in.	hot	6–7	9–10	12–15
	flank steak	whole	hot	4–5†		
	hamburger	1 in.	medium	3–4	5–6	7–10
	skewer		hot	4–5	6–8	10–12
Lamb	chops	1 in.	medium	5–6	7–8	10
	skewer		medium	5–6	7–8	10
Pork	chops	¾–1 in.	medium			18–20
	spareribs	whole	low/medium			1–1¼ hrs
	skewer		medium			15–20
Poultry	chicken	split	medium	5–6	10–11	35–45
	duck	split	medium			3

Veal	steaks or chops	1 in.	medium		9–12
	skewer		medium		10–15
Fish	steak	½ in.	medium		3–4
	steak	1 in.	medium		5–7
	fillets	¾ in.	medium		5–7
Lobster	split	1–1½ lb	medium/hot		14–15
Ham	slice	1 in.	medium		15–20

*If steaks are two inches or more thick you can use a meat thermometer. Steak is rare at 130°F, well-done at 170°F.

†Maximum cooking time for meat to be tender.

A good steel spit will be at least ¼ inch square, and should have two forks. Each fork should have two, and preferably four, sharp tines which will pierce and firmly hold the meat. It is important to ensure that the meat is properly balanced on the spit. Badly balanced meat will rotate in fits and starts, resulting in uneven cooking and heavy wear on the motor. With practice, you should be able to pass the spit through the centre of foods which have a uniform shape, such as a rolled roast. After skewering the meat on the spit, a balance test should be carried out.

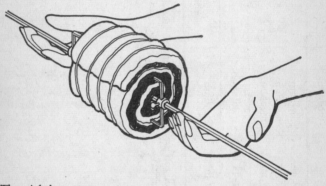

The spit balance test

Hold the spit as shown above and check its tendency to roll. Slowly rotate the spit on your palms and there should be no tendency to roll quickly from any position if the balance is even. If it does roll, re-skewer it to improve the balance, and if necessary use balancing weights to correct the drag. Very fat meat will shift its balance during cooking and may have to be re-spitted or balanced with a weight.

To safeguard against the spit forks working loose during cooking, tighten them with pliers.

It makes life easier for the cook if the drip pan can be placed to the front of the fire-bowl; the roast should therefore rotate away from the cook (see figure on p. 31 for placement of drip pan). Cooking efficiency can be slightly improved by fixing a sheet of aluminium foil (shiny side facing the spit) inside the barbecue hood.

Various barbecue accessories can be used in conjunction with the spit. Spit baskets, made from wire, are available in flat or cylindrical form: the flat basket is not deep enough to allow the food to turn over, whilst the cylindrical basket allows the food to 'tumble'. A shish-kebab attachment is useful for cooking several kebabs at one go and a hot dog wheel will impale up to a dozen sausages.

Smoke cooking

Smoke cooking should not be confused with smoke curing. Smoking as a way of preserving meat or fish is a slow process that takes several days and requires very little heat. Smoke cooking on the other hand uses the heat generated from the barbecue fuel to cook the food – completing the task in a similar time to an oven – and the smoke to impart flavour. It is only really effective in a covered barbecue. It is quite easy to use an effective drip pan right under the food, with the coals in a ring or on the side: heat and smoke are both trapped anyway. Smoke is produced by the addition of wood chips or twigs to the hot charcoal. Small quantities of dampened hardwood sawdust are fine, but not the sawdust from pine or other resinous softwoods as this will create an unpleasant flavour and ruin the food. Hickory and apple-wood chips are the most popular for making smoke and are generally available in small packs. Instructions for use are given on the pack, but should you decide to use home-made chips remember to soak them in water for about twenty minutes before placing them on the hot coals. The earlier the wood chips are put on the coals, the stronger the smoke flavour imparted to the food.

Spit-roasting time-chart

Food Type	Cut	Size or Weight	Recommended Fire-heat	Approximate Cooking Time in Hours*		
				rare	medium	well-done
				140°F	160°F	190°F
Beef	rump (rolled)	3–5 lb	medium	1½–2	2¼–3	3–4
	sirloin	5–6 lb	medium-hot	1¼–1¾	2¼–3	3–4
	rolled rib	4–6 lb	medium-hot	2–2½	2¼–3	3¼–4½
				140°F	160°F	180°F
Lamb	leg	3½–8 lb	medium	1–1¼	1½–2	2–3¼
	rolled shoulder	3–6 lb	medium	1–1¼	1½–2	2–3¼
						185°F
Pork	shoulder	3–6 lb	medium			2–3
	loin	3–5 lb	medium			2–3
	spareribs	2–4 lb	medium-hot			1–1¾
	fresh ham	5–8 lb	medium			3½–4½
						190°F
Poultry	chicken	2½–5 lb	medium			1–1½
	turkey	10–18 lb	medium			2–4

				190°F
Veal	leg	5–8 lb	medium	2–3
	rolled shoulder	3–5 lb	medium	$1\frac{1}{2}$–$2\frac{1}{2}$
	loin	5–6 lb	medium	$1\frac{1}{2}$–$2\frac{1}{4}$
				120–130°F
Fish	large, whole	5–10 lb	low-medium	$1\frac{1}{2}$–3
	small, whole	$1\frac{1}{2}$–4 lb	low-medium	$1\frac{1}{4}$–2

*For accuracy use a meat thermometer and cook to the internal temperatures given in the chart.

For a really strong flavour, it will be necessary to add more dampened chips to the fire as the smoke dies down.

The smell of the smoke can be masked by adding a few bay leaves, or sprigs of rosemary or thyme to the fire. Spareribs, ham, poultry, pork, fish and oysters are excellent for smoke cooking and baked beans placed in an open container will take on a pleasant smoky flavour, while the surface may become a little dry and crusty.

In the coals

To save space and cook more of a meal at one time, several things can be cooked directly in the fire-pan, either in the coals or on the side. Potatoes, whole aubergines, onions, securely wrapped in double foil, will cook here in the same way and the same time as in a rather hot oven.

In a fire-pit

Fire-pit cooking is strictly for very large parties: the preparation time is long, but the quantity you can cope with at one time is almost without limit.

Basically the fire-pit is a trench, dug to suit the requirements of the party you are catering for. In this trench a wood fire is lit and reduced to charcoal while heating the walls and the ground below. When ready (in about three to six hours) the fire-bed is covered with dry sand. The food, wrapped in foil and then covered with cloth which is liberally doused with water, is placed on the sand in as many layers as necessary. A metal grid may be put over it before the whole trench is filled up with closely packed earth, to a layer of at least a foot.

You then have a large Dutch oven, in which you can cook the hind-quarters of beef (dressed, some 100–150 pounds) in about fifteen hours. A 20-pound piece would take eight to ten hours, pots of beans four to six hours. Until you are an experienced fire-pit cook you can only guess at the time needed, but the odd hour more will not easily spoil the food, which is being steam-cooked in its own moisture. If you construct a more permanent fire-pit you can line the trench with brick or fire-stones (natural stone is rather hazardous with the temperatures involved) and put a grill in to build a better fire on. The trench should be longer than the grill on both sides to allow ventilation. Hardwood and fruit woods are the best fuel – do not burn just any old rubbish, for the smell will remain in the food. Once the pit has been closed, check at intervals for escaping steam and re-seal any outlets you might find.

8 Buying meat for the barbecue

Meat for barbecuing should be of the best quality you can afford and should be suitable for either roasting, grilling or frying. Meat-tenderizers, or the use of a good marinade, will enable you to barbecue less tender, and cheaper, cuts such as flank, blade and chuck, quite successfully.

Beef

The lean of good-quality beef should be bright red with a brownish tinge and be firm to the touch; it should be marbled with small streaks of white fat which helps to produce tenderness and flavour when the meat is cooked. Very lean meat is sometimes tough and rather flavourless. The colour of the outer covering of fat should be creamy, although at certain times of the year it can have a yellowish appearance.

Avoid buying beef that has a very dark colour and looks somewhat dry, as this indicates the meat has, in all probability, come from an old animal or, alternatively, has been exposed to the air for too long.

There are numerous ways of cutting a carcase but the names of the cuts given below are those most commonly used. Your butcher will be able to advise you of any local variations.

Fillet steak

The fillet is taken from the undercut of sirloin and is a very expensive, but very tender cut. Large pieces of fillet – they should weigh at least $2\frac{1}{2}$ lb – can be roasted and are easy to carve. Individual portions of 6–8 oz should be grilled.

Sirloin

With the bone in, a sirloin joint should weigh not less than $3\frac{1}{2}$–4 lb and should contain the undercut or fillet. Sirloin can be boned and rolled, but it has more flavour, and the meat is juicier, when roasted on the bone.

T-bone

Easily recognized by the shape of its bone, the T-bone steak is tender and has an excellent flavour. Ideally the steak should be $1\frac{1}{2}$–2 inches thick and weigh approximately $1\frac{1}{2}$ lb. T-bone steak one inch thick weighs about $\frac{3}{4}$ lb.

Rib steaks and roasts

Top rib, fore rib and back rib are all similar cuts – the chief difference between them being the length of the rib bones. Fore rib, with the longest bones, can be made into a separate joint by cutting off the rib ends. Ribs can be grilled as they are or boned and rolled for spit cooking. A one-inch thick rib steak weighs about 1 lb. The generous marbling of fat in these steaks give them a very good flavour.

Flank

Flank varies in thickness according to which part of the animal's belly the cut is taken from. Thick flank is suitable for slow roasting and can be rolled for spit cooking. Flank has a strong flavour and is quite lean with rather coarse fibres.

Porterhouse

A tender and excellently flavoured steak, the porterhouse is a $1\frac{1}{2}$–2-inch slice taken from the wing rib. A $1\frac{1}{2}$-inch steak will weigh about 2 lb and should serve three to four people – although it is not as easy to carve as sirloin.

Rump

Rump steak is considered to have the best flavour of all the steak cuts, but to be tender it must be well hung. One indication of this is its colour; the lean should have purplish tinge and the fat should be a creamy white. A large piece of rump, weighing 4–6 lb, can be rolled, tied and spit roasted and will serve twelve to eighteen people. A one-inch-thick slice will weigh about $1\frac{1}{2}$ lb and serve three or four people.

Chuck

Of fairly good flavour, chuck is a lean cut with very little, if any, fat. Unless the chuck steak is marinated and/or treated with a meat tenderizer, it will require long, slow cooking.

Lamb

Lean good-quality lamb will vary from a light pink, for a very young lamb, to a fairly dark red for a mature sheep. A layer of fat should cover the legs and shoulders, and both of these joints should have a plump look about them. The colour of the fat will vary according to the origin of the animal. Home-produced lamb – only available from the butcher during the spring and early summer – will have creamy white fat and the fat of imported lamb will be white. Avoid buying lamb whose fat is yellowish and rather brittle as this will indicate either an old animal or one that has spent too long in the freezer.

Shoulder

Not a particularly good joint for barbecuing because the large proportion of bone to meat makes it rather extravagant. If you do want to barbecue shoulder, it should be boned and rolled or cut into small, boneless pieces for grilling or using for kebabs.

Leg

Unlike shoulder, leg of lamb has a large proportion of meat to bone. The best part of the leg for barbecuing is the fillet (top end). The leg can be spit roasted whole or after being boned, rolled and tied. Alternatively, the leg can be boned, the halves opened up and cooked directly on the grill.

Chops

Ideally the chops bought for barbecuing should be about $1\frac{1}{2}$ inch thick with the minimum of bone. Loin or chump chops are therefore better than rib chops, and are particularly suitable for grilling. Another good cut is a steak or 'chop' from the leg.

Pork

The flesh of a young animal should be fine textured and pink. The meat of older animals is coarser and of a darker colour. The skin hould feel smooth and firm to the touch and the meat of a young pig will contain very little gristle. Cut flesh should be slightly moist and contain small flecks of fat. The bones of a young animal should be small and pinkish in colour. Bones of older animals are an off-white colour.

Leg

The hind leg of the pig, weighing 10–12 lb, can be barbecued whole or cut up into steaks or chops. When wet-cured in a brine solution the hind leg, or sometimes the fore leg, becomes gammon and may be smoked or unsmoked (green). Unsmoked gammon is milder in flavour than smoked.

Ham

This comes from the hind leg and is 'dry cured' (much more slowly than gammon) in a mixture of salt-petre and salt. Some experts do not recommend roasting smoked cured ham over charcoal but there is no harm in doing so if you stick to recommended cooking times and temperatures. Tinned cooked ham can be barbecued and will only require a few minutes grilling to warm through and become lightly browned.

Loin

The loin is the best and most expensive joint. The whole loin, weighing 12–14 lb, is usually cut into chops or several roasts. The choice centre cut, weighing about 4–5 lb, can be boned, rolled and tied for cooking on the spit.

Sparerib

Sparerib is probably the best known and most popular cut of pork for barbecuing. The joint, which is fairly lean, comes from the area immediately behind the head and has a broad cut area where the blade, fore leg and hand have been sliced away. Allow about ¾ lb per serving.

Chops

The most tender, best-flavoured and expensive chops come from the loin. Neck and chump chops are also suitable for grilling.

Hand and spring (fore leg)

An awkwardly shaped joint which can be boned, rolled and tied for spit cooking, or boned and cut into small pieces for grilling or using for kebabs.

Veal

The least satisfactory meat for barbecuing, since it is very lean and has a tendency to become dry when cooked over a charcoal fire; its delicate flavour can be somewhat over-powered by the charcoal smoke.

Veal from milk-fed calves is very tender and considered superior to grass-fed veal although the latter has more flavour. The flesh of good-quality veal should be a very pale pink or off white from milk-fed calves and a pale pink from grass-fed calves. The flesh should have a fine texture and be moist and soft – but not too flabby or wet. Flesh that has either a dry, pale brown or bluish appearance will be stale. Veal bones are pinkish white and very soft in comparison to those of mature animals. There is very little external fat and its colour will vary from pinkish white to a pale yellow tinge. The fat around the kidneys should be firm and very white.

An important point to consider, before buying veal for a barbecue, is that it keeps very badly and should be used within a few days of slaughter. It would therefore be wise to check with your butcher that he will have veal available when you need it.

Leg

The leg can be cooked complete with the bone or boned and rolled.

Shoulder

Although the shoulder can be roasted on the bone, its awkward shape usually results in it being boned, rolled and stuffed.

Chops

Usually cut from the loin. Chump chops have a round bone in their centre and are cut from the bottom end of the loin. They can be grilled.

9 Basic instructions for barbecuing meat and fish

Cooking steaks on an open grill

Top-quality steaks are the best for barbecuing – a tender cut from the ribs or loin such as T-bone, sirloin, rib, porterhouse and fillet. Steaks and other small cuts are cooked by the direct-heat method (p. 56). When using a cheaper cut of steak, which will be less tender, marinate the meat before barbecuing. Marinating will tenderize the meat and give it a distinctive flavour. The longer a steak is marinated, the stronger the flavour. Some marinade recipes are given in Chapter 12. Steaks should be removed from the refrigerator or freezer in good time to allow them to thaw and reach room temperature. Generally speaking, steaks taken from a refrigerator will take at least an hour to reach room temperature.

Solid-fat edging should be slashed at 1–1½ inch intervals almost into the lean – doing this keeps the steak from curling. Alternatively, you can trim off the excess fat to within ⅛-inch of the lean meat.

Allow 10–15 minutes per side (including searing time) to cook 1½–2-inch-thick steaks rare. Allow 2–3 minutes per side longer for medium and a further 3–4 minutes for well done.

If steaks are 2 inches or more thick you can use a meat thermometer. Steak is rare at 130°F, medium at 150°F, well done at 170°F.

Unless your taste is for meat cooked evenly throughout,

steaks should never be turned more than once. The first side will be cooked to a rare condition when droplets of bright red juices rise on the uncooked side, and the second side will be rare when juices begin to bubble from the top side.

If in doubt about the readiness of a steak, cut into it (preferably along the bone if it has one) to check the inside colour. A rare steak is browned on the outside and still bright red (but not raw) on the inside. When medium done, the inside is a duller red, but still juicy. It is well done just when the inside red turns to brown – with most of the juices still in it.

Seasoning

Salt draws out the meat juices so it is best to add salt when the steak is cooked and on the plate. Basting with prepared sauces, especially those with a strong flavour, should be carried out during the last few minutes of grilling otherwise the sauce flavour may swamp the steak's natural flavour. Cracked peppercorns can be pressed into the steak before barbecuing or it can be rubbed with a cut clove of garlic.

Marinated steaks should not require seasoning after barbecuing. Unless you know your guests' taste, it is safer to salt and pepper very lightly, if at all, and not to baste.

Barbecuing steaks for a crowd

The problem of cooking a variety of rare, medium and well-done steaks for a crowd can be solved by the way you arrange the prepared coals. When the briquets are ready, pile most at the front of the grill, leaving a few scattered ones at the back. Start your well-done steaks at front. Sear first sides – then cook about half the time normally required and slide steaks to back of grill. Next, sear and cook the medium-done steaks at the front in the same manner, also allowing about half the normal cooking time. When these are ready slide them to back of grill – at the same time turning the well-done steaks already there. Now cook the rare steaks at the front of grill. Cook the first sides completely and turn – at the same time turning the medium done steaks at the back of the grill. When the second sides of rare steaks are completed, remove them from the grill – then, in turn, remove the medium-done and, lastly, the well-done steaks. If you often cook for a crowd it is very useful to have a hooded grill that incorporates a warming oven, but remember that the steaks will continue cooking whilst in the oven even though not subject to direct heat from the briquets.

Beef roasts on an open grill

All roasts are cooked by the reflected heat method (see p. 56). Cuts such as rump and chuck are much improved by marinating or basting with a sauce. Unsecured pieces from a rolled roast must be trussed with twine to prevent burning.

A roast is cooking when its juices are visibly bubbling, but the best way to determine the exact readiness of barbecued

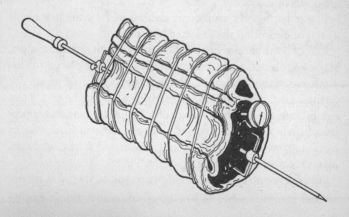

roast is to use a meat thermometer. See p. 42 and the chart on p. 66.

Rib roasts

The roast must be prepared by sawing through the ribs about two inches from their ends. Remove the small pieces of rib and fold the flap of meat over the rib ends. Then saw through the back bones to open up a wedge and insert a piece of suet. Tie the roast with twine at approximately one-inch intervals to produce a cylindrical shape. Insert the spit diagonally through the meaty section.

Lamb – chops, leg and shoulder

Lamb chops and steaks are barbecued by direct heat in the same manner as beef steaks. Most people prefer lamb when it is medium done (faded pink inside). Marinating is unnecessary; seasoning with salt and freshly ground pepper after the chops are done should be adequate.

Leg of lamb and shoulder are cooked in the same manner as a joint of beef using the reflected heat method.

Leg of lamb should be spit roasted whole to retain its juices. Have your butcher saw about three inches of the bone off the small end of the leg, leaving the meat to form a flap which can be folded over the bone and and held in place by the spit. Then rub oil into the meat, make small incisions and insert peppercorns, herbs or garlic slivers if you wish. The meat should be medium to well done throughout (roast lamb is best when the meat thermometer registers 170–180°F).

If you have no spit for roasting large joints, the meat should be turned fairly frequently, say every 5–10 minutes, and basted each time it is turned. Allow approximately thirty minutes per pound cooking time – but do watch the meat thermometer.

Pork – chops and roasts

Pork chops and steaks are cooked in the same manner as beef steaks, and the pork roast in the same manner as a beef roast. Pork must never be served rare; it should be medium to well-done. When sufficiently done, the meat will be white to grey in colour and the meat thermometer should read at least 185°F.

Spareribs

These should be impaled through the meaty portion between the ribs in concertina fashion and the ends of the piece firmly held by the fork tines.

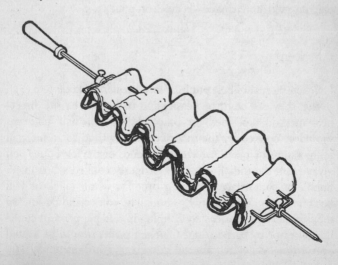

Ham

The shape and weight of a whole ham make it advisable to cut the ham in half diagonally and balance one half against the other.

Ready-to-eat ham has already been sufficiently cooked and barbecuing is, therefore, mainly used to improve the flavour. It should not be cooked beyond an internal temperature of about 140°F. Hams which are uncooked, or smoked or tenderized, require thorough cooking to an internal temperature of 185°F. The meat should pull away from the bone when done. Cook in the same manner as a beef or pork roast – by reflected heat – allowing about twelve minutes per pound for a ready-to-eat ham and about twenty-five minutes per pound for an uncooked one. Before barbecuing remove the rind from the ham. It is customary to score the fat in a diamond pattern and then to stick whole cloves into the centres of the diamonds. Baste generously during the last 20–30 minutes of cooking with a marinade – recipes on pp. 131–5.

Chicken

Chicken pieces are best put in a wire broiler basket (see p. 43). so that they can be turned easily and barbecued by the direct-heat method described on p. 56. Whole or half chickens should be cooked by the reflected heat method to an internal temperature of 190°F (or when the ends of the leg bones pull away from the meat). They are properly cooked when juices bubble on the surface. Cooking time for whole chickens will be about 25–30 minutes per pound. The colour and flavour of the skin can be enhanced by rubbing in salt, pepper and cooking oil prior to barbecuing. Chicken pieces should be basted every time they are turned (every 3–4 minutes). Whole chickens or halves, can be basted at intervals if required, but this is not necessary if you are using a spit. For basting use cooking oil, butter, margarine or a suitable sauce.

It will prove more economical, when barbecuing for a crowd, to buy chicken pieces rather than cut up whole chickens.

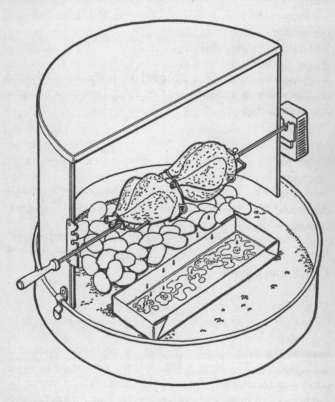

Small birds can be spitted two or more at a time, placed closely together and firmly trussed. The spit rod should pass through the neck and just above the tail of each bird and the fork tines should be fixed at each end of the line of birds.

Legs and wings should be trussed with twine to prevent burning.

Large capons or turkeys, because of their extra weight, are best spitted by running the spit rod in at a slight diagonal through the neck flap (just below the breast bone) and out just above the tail.

Turkey

A whole turkey is spit-barbecued in the same manner as chicken, using the reflected-heat method. Drumsticks may be treated as chicken pieces.

Duck

Duck should be barbecued in the same manner as a chicken. Because of the greater amount of fat in a duck, it takes approximately half as long again to barbecue. Duck does not require basting and should preferably be served with a well-flavoured sauce. Whole birds are cooked at about 190°F internal temperature.

Rabbit

Disjoint the rabbit and barbecue in the same manner as chicken pieces. The meat is done when it pulls away from the bones – at about 180°F internal temperature. To prevent the meat from drying, it is necessary to baste frequently, or alternatively, wrap in pieces of bacon which you skewer in place.

Sausages and frankfurters

Generally speaking, sausages require the same cooking time as the meat they contain. Continental sausages, such as the German bratwurst, are delicious when barbecued for about 15 minutes or so – turning only once. Frankfurters are pre-cooked and only need to be warmed and browned to bring out their flavour.

To prevent sausages from bursting, it is advisable to prick them to allow fat to drain off during barbecuing. Skewering a sausage from end to end will prevent it curling and make it easier to handle. Scoring a sausage diagonally at half-inch intervals will also prevent it from curling.

Fish

Many fish can be barbecued successfully. Fish must always be fully cooked, but do not make the mistake of over cooking as this will result in dryness and loss of flavour. Fish is properly cooked when the internal temperature is 140–145°F (maximum).

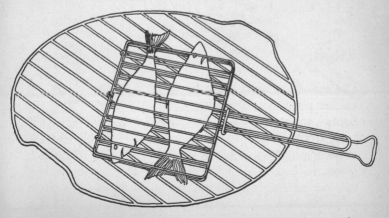

At this point it will flake easily. To prepare a whole fish, clean it thoroughly. The head can be removed or left on. Small fish can be scaled and served in their skins. Large fish can be barbecued with the scales on and skinned afterwards. Scaled fish should have their skin thoroughly rubbed with melted butter and lemon juice. This mixture can be blended with vinegar, garlic, wine and herbs according to taste. If the scales are left on, the mixture can be used to season the inside of the fish before sewing up the cavity. Alternatively, the cavity can be stuffed with breadcrumbs flavoured with the mixture.

Small fish, and fish steaks, are best held in a spit basket or a wire broiler. Large fish may be skewered on a spit (see below) or placed on the grill using the reflected-heat method. Since

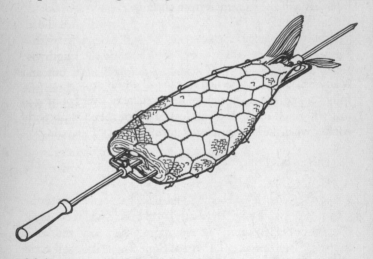

fish becomes very delicate and easily broken when cooked, it is a good idea to wrap the fish in a clean piece of chicken wire, securing it tightly around the length of the fish. Remember to oil the basket, broiler or grill first to prevent sticking. Another excellent way to cook fish on the grill is to wrap it in aluminium foil.

Allow 10–15 minutes total time for small fish or steaks and 7–9 minutes per pound for a large fish. In any event, it is best to check frequently after the minimum time. If the fish is wrapped in aluminium foil, allow 20 per cent more cooking time. Fish barbecued on an open grill should be turned over three times at equally spaced intervals, basting each time.

Lobster

Whole live lobsters (and they must be alive when purchased) and lobster tails are particularly delicious when barbecued.

To clean the lobster yourself, lay it on its back on a cutting board. Insert the tip of a sharp-pointed knife between the tail section and the body shell. Cut through the spinal cord and all the way through to the back shell. Crack the claws with a hammer or heavy mallet. Then with a knife slit lengthwise along the thin under-shell from head to tail. Lift out and discard the dark vein down the centre and the small sac (the stomach), about two inches long, just below the head. If you don't want to try this yourself have the fishmonger prepare it for you, but remember the lobster must be as fresh as possible when you cook it. The cavity can be stuffed with a mixture of finely chopped celery, apple and parsley. Brush generously with melted butter – salt and pepper to taste.

Use the direct-heat method and start barbecuing with the shell side down. Brush frequently with butter whilst cooking. Allow about 15 minutes cooking time then turn and cook about 5 minutes more. Lobster is done when the shell turns a bright red.

Recipes

10 Cooking on the grill and a few roasts

Grilled trout   Serves 4

4 trout (about ¾ lb each)

Marinade

3 tablespoons olive oil

1 medium size onion finely chopped

1 teaspoon French mustard

1 tablespoon minced chives

2 tablespoons minced dill

1 teaspoon salt

1 tablespoon lemon juice

½ teaspoon pepper

2 tablespoons melted butter

herb butter (p. 139)

Clean and bone the trout and if desired, remove the heads. Flatten the fish out and place them flesh side down, in a shallow dish.

Combine oil, onion, mustard, chives, dill, salt, lemon juice and pepper and mix thoroughly. Pour this marinade over the fish and put in the refrigerator for about an hour, turning fish once.

Place the fish, flesh side down, on an oiled grill over medium/hot coals and cook for about 4 minutes. Turn the fish over and brush melted butter over the upper side. Continue grilling for another 7–8 minutes or until the skin of the trout is crisp and the flesh is white and can easily be flaked.

Spread the herb butter over the fish just before serving.

Grilled stuffed trout   Serves 4

4 trout (about 8–10 oz each)   ½ teaspoon salt
4 oz walnuts, finely chopped   1 egg
2 tablespoons lemon juice   1 tablespoon vegetable oil
2 tablespoons minced parsley   lemon wedges

Clean the trout, keeping the head and tail intact. Wash the fish thoroughly and pat dry with paper towels.

Mix the walnuts, lemon juice, parsley and salt together and bind with the egg. Stuff each of the fish with the mixture (about 3 tablespoons per fish) and close the openings with fine metal skewers or cocktail sticks.

Brush oil on both sides of the fish and place the fish on an oiled grill which is positioned 5–6 inches above hot coals. Allow about 6 minutes for each side of the trout or until the flesh can be easily flaked with a fork.

Serve with lemon wedges.

Grilled stuffed crab   Serves 6

1 lb crab meat   ¼ teaspoon salt
4 tablespoons melted butter   pinch of cayenne pepper
1 oz finely chopped parsley   6 crab shells
2 tablespoons lemon juice   lemon wedges

Carefully check that the crab meat is free of shell pieces or cartilage. Wash the shells and grease the insides with butter or margarine.

Combine and blend together the crab meat, butter, parsley, lemon juice, salt and cayenne pepper. Divide the mixture into six equal portions and stuff the prepared shells. Wrap each crab shell in two sheets of heavy-duty aluminium foil. Place on the grill over hot coals and barbecue for about 15 minutes or until shells turn brown.

Garnish with more chopped parsley and serve with lemon wedges.

Grilled fish steaks   Serves 4

4 fresh or frozen halibut or haddock steaks, 1–1½ inches thick	3 oz melted butter
	½ teaspoon salt
	¼ teaspoon pepper
seafare marinade (p. 133)	1 tablespoon lemon juice

Place the fish in a shallow dish. Pour the marinade over the fish and let stand for about half an hour, turning once.

Tear off four pieces of 18-inch heavy-duty aluminium foil and brush melted butter on the polished surface of each piece. Place a portion of fish on each of the buttered surfaces and sprinkle with salt and pepper. Combine the remainder of the melted butter with the lemon juice and brush over the fish. Fold the foil over and secure the edges tightly.

Place the packages on the grill over medium coals and cook for approximately 20 minutes or until the fish flakes easily with a fork.

Open the foil during the last 5 minutes of cooking time to allow the barbecue smoke to flavour the fish.

Garlic steak   Serves 4

4 steaks	1 tablespoon fresh chopped parsley
1 clove garlic	
2 oz softened butter	

Rub both sides of the meat with a freshly cut garlic clove and put to one side. Prepare garlic butter (for the garnish) as follows: finely mince the pieces of cut garlic and blend well into the softened butter with the fresh chopped parsley. Brush the steak lightly on both sides with oil or a little melted butter and barbecue over hot coals according to taste.

Serve topped with a pat of the garlic butter.

Red wine steak   Serves 4

4 steaks	$\frac{1}{4}$ cup water
1 oz butter or margarine	$\frac{3}{4}$ cup red wine
1 tablespoon finely chopped onion	salt and pepper
	2 tablespoons fresh chopped
1 tablespoon flour	parsley

Brush the meat lightly on both sides with melted butter and barbecue over hot coals according to taste. Transfer to a hot dish and serve with sauce made as follows: sauté the onion in melted butter in a frying pan until golden brown. Mix the flour and water until smooth and add to the frying pan together with the red wine. Bring to the boil, stirring continuously. Season to taste, and simmer for 10 minutes, adding parsley immediately before serving.

The sauce can be prepared ahead and re-heated on the barbecue during the time the steaks are being grilled.

Steak au poivre flambé   Serves 4

4 steaks, approximately $\frac{3}{4}$ inch thick	2 oz butter or margarine
	oregano
2 tablespoons black peppercorns	pinch garlic salt
	4 tablespoons brandy
2 large tomatoes	

Crush the peppercorns coarsely with a rolling pin and press into both sides of the meat. Allow the meat to stand at room temperature for approximately 30 minutes to absorb the flavour.

Barbecue over hot coals to the required degree and transfer it to a hot dish. Thickly slice the tomatoes and sauté in melted butter in a frying pan until the slices are hot through. Season with oregano and garlic salt to taste. Arrange the tomato slices on top of the steak. Warm the brandy, ignite and spoon, flaming, over the meat.

Sirloin with anchovy Serves 4–6

2½ lb sirloin steak, cut about   2 oz anchovy fillets
   1½ inches thick   3 oz stuffed olives
1 oz butter   dash of pepper
1 teaspoon anchovy paste

Blend the butter with the anchovy paste. Barbecue the steak over hot coals for approximately 7 minutes. Turn it and spread the blended butter over the grilled surface. Continue barbecuing the steak for about 6–8 minutes, or until cooked to the required degree.

Remove it to a carving board. Arrange the anchovy fillets across the top of the steak in a criss-cross pattern and place a sliced stuffed olive in the centre of each diamond shape. Carve into slices about one inch thick, and serve immediately.

Rosemary-smoked sirloin Serves 10–12

1 top sirloin steak (boneless)   or 2 teaspoons dried
   cut 2 inches thick   rosemary
   (approximately 4½ lb)   salt
1½ tablespoons fresh rosemary   pepper

Press equal proportions of the rosemary into both sides of the steak. Barbecue steak over medium coals in a covered barbecue – or if your barbecue does not have a cover, refer to the

instructions for making a hood from aluminium foil, on
p. 32. Each side of steak should receive the same amount of
cooking time (about 15 minutes each side for rare meat).
Season the steak with salt and pepper and slice it across the
grain.

Cowboy steak   Serves 6–8

6–8 steaks at least one inch
  thick (total weight about
  4 lb)
1 cup (about ½ pint) bacon
  dripping
4 tablespoons lemon juice
6 tablespoons finely chopped
  onions

1 tablespoon Worcestershire
  sauce
1 tablespoon horseradish
  sauce
½ teaspoon salt
⅛ teaspoon pepper
1 teaspoon paprika
1 clove garlic, minced
2 bay leaves

Place the steaks in a single layer in a shallow pan. Melt the
bacon dripping in a saucepan. Add lemon juice, chopped
onions, Worcestershire sauce, horseradish sauce, salt, pepper,
paprika, garlic and bay leaves. Stir thoroughly, and pour over
the meat. Allow the steaks to marinate for about 30 minutes,
turning them once during that period. Remove the steaks from
the marinade, drain off the excess liquid and barbecue over
hot coals.

Texas short ribs   Serves 4–6

2–3 lb lean short ribs (about
  3 inches long)
1 teaspoon salt
1 tablespoon brown sugar

½ pint tomato juice
¼ teaspoon cloves
⅛ teaspoon thyme
1 teaspoon dry mustard

1 clove garlic, minced
(optional)
6 tablespoons dry red wine
1 teaspoon Worcestershire
sauce

3 tablespoons olive oil
3 tablespoons onions, finely
chopped

Place the meat in a shallow pan. Combine all the seasoning
ingredients – except the oil and onions – and pour over the
meat. Refrigerate for 24–48 hours, turning occasionally. Allow
the meat to warm to room temperature before cooking. About
30 minutes before you start cooking, add the oil and onions to
the marinade. Grease the grill, and set it about 4 inches above
the hot coals. Cook the ribs for 30–40 minutes during which
time they should be basted and turned every 10 minutes. It
will help to retain moisture in the ribs if a loose sheet of foil
is placed over them during cooking. Any marinade left over
can be boiled and spooned over the cooked short ribs when
serving.

Blue-cheese steak   Serves 4–6

1 whole flank steak (about
1½ lb)
½ pint well-seasoned French
dressing
3 tablespoons butter or
margarine

6 tablespoons blue cheese
¾ tablespoon chives, chopped
1 clove garlic, minced
1½ tablespoons brandy

Place the steak in a shallow baking dish, cover with the French
dressing and marinate for several hours. Prepare blue-cheese
butter by creaming butter and cheese until blended. Mix in
the chives, garlic and brandy. If the butter is prepared ahead
and kept in the refrigerator, warm it to room temperature
before using.

Remove the steak from the marinade and barbecue over hot

coals, allowing 5 minutes each side for rare steak. Slice the meat, diagonally, into $\frac{1}{8}$–$\frac{1}{4}$-inch-thick strips. Spoon the blue-cheese butter over the meat and serve immediately.

Beef-strip teriyaki   Serves 5–6

1 whole flank steak (about 1$\frac{1}{2}$ lb)
$\frac{1}{2}$ pint beef consommé (undiluted)*
4 tablespoons soy sauce
1$\frac{1}{2}$ teaspoons seasoned salt
3 tablespoons finely chopped spring onions
1 clove garlic, minced
2 tablespoons lime juice
1$\frac{3}{4}$ tablespoons honey or brown sugar

Cut the flank steak into $\frac{3}{8}$-inch slices across the grain. Place the strips in a shallow baking dish. Prepare a marinade by combining beef consommé, soy sauce, seasoned salt, onions, garlic, lime juice and honey or brown sugar. Pour the marinade over meat and refrigerate overnight turning occasionally. Drain the meat and retain the marinade.

The strips can be cooked flat on the grill or threaded, accordion style, on skewers. Grill them quickly over hot coals, giving each side about 2 minutes, basting with the marinade. They should only be turned once.

* If you prefer, mix $\frac{1}{4}$ pint consommé with an equal quantity of dry red or white wine.

Individual steak packet   Individual serving

6–8 oz round steak
1 tablespoon flour
heavy–duty aluminium foil
1 medium-size carrot cut into strips
1 small onion, quartered
1 small potato, peeled and cut into strips
2 slices (rings) of green pepper
4 tablespoons chopped celery

½ teaspoon salt
2 tablespoons tomato sauce
pinch of pepper

1 tablespoon of dry red wine
(or water)

Pound the flour into the steak and put it on the aluminium foil. Arrange the various vegetables on and around the steak. Top with the remaining ingredients. Sprinkle the food with the wine (or water). Fold the foil over and seal the edges. Put the package on the grill, positioned about 4 inches above medium coals, and cook for 30–40 minutes – turning every 10 minutes or so. The steak and vegetables can be eaten direct from the foil.

Packet steak   Serves 4–6

2 lb round steak one inch
  thick
1 teaspoon salt
¼ teaspoon pepper
1 teaspoon paprika
3 tablespoons flour
2 tablespoons bacon fat

½ pint tomato sauce
1 medium-size onion – sliced
½ teaspoon garlic salt
6 tablespoons chopped green
  pepper
heavy-duty aluminium foil

Mix the salt, pepper, paprika and flour and pound the mixture into the steak with a mallet. Place a heavy frying pan on the grill and heat. When sufficiently hot pour in the bacon fat and quickly sauté the steak until browned on both sides. Combine the tomato sauce with the remaining ingredients, and spoon half of the mixture into centre of the piece of foil. Place the steak on top of the mixture, and pour over the rest of the sauce. Fold foil over and seal the edges. Place the package on the grill over medium coals, and cook for 1½ hours, or until the meat is tender. Turn the package several times with tongs. A few minutes before the steak is ready, open up the sealed edges to allow the meat to absorb some of the charcoal flavour. The juice n the foil should be served with the steak.

Steak in a crust   Serves 6

6 steaks, approximately
    4 inches square and about
    one inch thick
meat tenderizer (preferably
    unseasoned)
salad oil
garlic salt

12 oz plain flour
2 teaspoons salt
2 oz margarine
2 oz lard
approximately $\frac{1}{4}$ pint cold
    water

Prepare the steaks by using meat tenderizer (follow instructions). Brush salad oil on to all meat surfaces and sprinkle generously with garlic salt. Lay meat to one side and prepare the pastry.

Sift together the flour and salt. Rub in the fats until the mixture resembles fine breadcrumbs. Stir in sufficient water to make a stiff dough. Roll out the dough on a lightly floured surface until approximately $\frac{1}{8}$-inch thick. Cut six pieces of pastry approximately 8 inches square. Put a piece of steak on one half of the pastry square; fold the pastry over the meat, moisten the edges with milk and seal together. Prick the pastry with a fork.

Cook the steak pies on a grill set about 5 inches above medium coals, for about 40 minutes, turning them occasionally.

Providing it is not too charred, most people will probably eat the crust with the steak.

London broil with piquant sauce   Serves 4–6

2$\frac{1}{4}$ lb piece of skirt of beef

Marinade
4 tablespoons Worcestershire
    sauce
2 tablespoons oil

4 tablespoons water
juice of half a lemon
salt

Sauce

3 oz butter	6 gherkins, chopped
2 teaspoons prepared English mustard	2 tablespoons double cream

Combine all the marinade ingredients in a shallow dish. Immerse the beef in the marinade and leave in the refrigerator for at least 12 hours, turning once.

Melt the butter, remove from the heat and stir in the remaining sauce ingredients. Leave to cool.

Remove the meat from the marinade and pierce lengthways with a long skewer. Spread with a little sauce and place on the oiled grill about 5 inches above hot coals.

Cook for 10 minutes on each side if you want the meat rare, longer if it is to be well done. Spread with more sauce two or three times during cooking.

To carve, place on a board and cut slightly at an angle into thin slices.

Rolled skirt with red wine sauce   Serves 6

6 pieces of skirt, rolled and secured with skewers (preferably made from wood)	1 small onion, chopped
	2 oz butter or margarine
	4 tablespoons red wine
6 oz thinly sliced mushrooms	$\frac{1}{2}$ teaspoon salt
3 oz chicken livers, chopped	pinch of black pepper
	sprig of parsley

Barbecue the skirt rolls over medium coals, with the grill set at 4–5 inches, for about 7 minutes on each side. Whilst the meat is cooking, sauté the mushrooms, chicken livers and onion in the butter until onion is tender. Add the wine, salt and pepper, and quickly bring to the boil. Continue boiling for about 3 minutes to reduce the liquid.

To serve, pour the sauce over the skirt rolls and garnish with the parsley.

Veal chops with white wine   Serves 6

6 veal chops, about one inch thick	6 tablespoons melted butter or margarine
4 tablespoons white wine	½ lemon – thinly sliced
¾ tablespoon paprika	salt and pepper to taste

Brush each chop on both sides with the white wine and sprinkle with paprika. Let the chops stand for about 40–50 minutes. Brush each one well with melted butter before placing them on the grill (grease the grill beforehand to prevent the chops sticking to it). Cook slowly over coals of a low temperature for about 20–30 minutes, frequently brushing the chops with melted butter. Turn only once – using tongs – and about 5 minutes before serving top with a slice of lemon.

Veal cutlets   Serves 4–6

2 lb veal neck cutlets, about one inch thick	juice of 2 lemons
2 tablespoons parsley, minced	1 tablespoon shallots, minced
½ clove garlic, crushed	salt and pepper
4 tablespoons salad oil	shallot butter (p. 139)

Mix together the parsley, garlic, oil, lemon juice, shallots, salt and pepper. Marinate the cutlets in this mixture for 2–3 hours, turning them frequently. Drain and place the cutlets on an oiled grill set about 4 inches above medium coals.

Cook for about 25 minutes, turning the cutlets once or twice and basting every 2–3 minutes with the remainder of the marinade. Serve with shallot butter.

Sweet and sour spareribs   Serves 6–10

4–6 lb lean spareribs
1 teaspoon salt
3 tablespoons soy sauce
3 tablespoons olive oil
¼ pint wine vinegar
5 oz brown sugar

6 tablespoons water
6 tablespoons pineapple juice
1 teaspoon grated fresh
  ginger (or ¼ teaspoon
  powdered ginger)

Rub the spareribs thorough'y with salt. Then put them directly on to the grill, or thread them on to the spit. If you use the grill it should be raised to approximately 6 inches above medium coals and the ribs turned every 10 minutes.

After cooking for 30–40 minutes start brushing the combined seasoning ingredients over the ribs and carry on cooking for another 30–40 minutes or until ribs are done (meat will pull away from end of rib bones). Basting and turning should be a continuous process to ensure even flavouring and to prevent the ribs being charred. Serve with a pineapple garnish and, if you like, an additional sweet and sour sauce.

Sparerib cutlets   Serves 4

8 sparerib pork cutlets
1 tablespoon mustard
1 tablespoon brown sugar

1 tablespoon melted butter
salt and pepper
2 oz chopped cashew nuts

Combine mustard, brown sugar, melted butter, salt and pepper, and spread over cutlets. Place them on an oiled grill set about 4 inches above hot coals and cook for approximately 20 minutes. Sprinkle chopped nuts over the cutlets and barbecue for another 5 minutes or so or until the nuts are golden brown.

Spiced orange glazed spareribs   Serves 4

3 lb meaty spareribs

Marinade and glaze
2 tablespoons clear honey
juice of ½ lemon
finely grated rind of ½ orange

juice of 2 oranges
2 tablespoons
   Worcestershire sauce
1 teaspoon soy sauce
salt

Combine all the marinade ingredients in a pan and heat gently. Simmer for 2 minutes. Cool. Cut the spareribs into serving pieces and place in a shallow dish. Pour over the marinade and leave for 12–24 hours, turning occasionally.

Remove the spareribs and place in a roasting pan. Reserve the marinade. Roast the spareribs at 350°F, gas mark 4, for one hour. When required, place them on an oiled grill set about 4 inches above the hot coals. Brush with the marinade and turn frequently. Cook for about 12–15 minutes until well glazed and crisp.

Spanish lamb steaks   Serves 6

6 lamb shoulder steaks, or
   chops, approximately one
   inch thick
2 tablespoons finely chopped
   onions
3 tablespoons tarragon wine
   vinegar

6 tablespoons olive, or salad,
   oil
1 bay leaf
½ teaspoon oregano
½ teaspoon black pepper
¾ teaspoon basil
9 tablespoons dry sherry

Place the meat in a shallow pan. Mix the remaining ingredients together and pour over the meat. Marinate overnight in the refrigerator, or for 2–4 hours at room temperature. Turn periodically. If taken from the refrigerator allow the meat to stand at room temperature for at least one hour before cooking. Drain the lamb steaks well and barbecue over hot coals for 20–35 minutes, turning frequently and basting with the marinade. Heat any marinade remaining and serve with the steaks.

Breast of lamb   Serves 4–6

3–4 lb breast of lamb
2 tablespoons sugar
½ pint orange juice
5 tablespoons lemon juice

2 oz finely chopped mint
  leaves
3 tablespoons salad oil

Marinate the breast of lamb overnight in a mixture of the sugar, orange juice and lemon juice. About 2 hours or so prior to cooking the meat add the mint leaves to the marinade.

Liberally oil the meat and barbecue over medium coals until thoroughly browned. Occasionally baste the meat during cooking with a sauce made from mixing 6 tablespoons of the marinade mixed with 3 tablespoons of salad oil.

The remainder of the marinade can be heated and served as a sauce with the meat.

Pan barbecued bacon

Because of its high fat content, bacon is not particularly suitable for cooking directly on the grill as fat dripping on to the charcoal is likely to cause flare-ups. The best way to overcome this is to barbecue the bacon in a frying pan. If you don't have a frying pan to hand, it is a simple matter to shape a pan from double-thickness aluminium foil.

The charcoal flavour will be more readily imparted to the bacon if the pan is loosely covered with an overlapping piece of foil.

Liver and bacon rolls   Serves 4

2 lb calf's liver (cut into 4 pieces approximately one inch thick)
8 rashers of lean bacon

Marinade
¼ pint olive oil   pinch of garlic salt
pinch of pepper

Trim the veins and outer skin from the liver and soak it in a salt-water solution (1 teaspoon of salt to 1 pint of water) for about 25 minutes. Remove the liver from the water and pat dry with a paper towel. Place a bacon rasher on top of, and underneath, each piece of liver. Roll up and secure with a skewer.

Combine the marinade ingredients in a shallow dish. Marinate the liver in a refrigerator for about 3 hours, turning twice during that time.

Barbecue the liver over medium coals for approximately 15 minutes, turning only once. It should not be overcooked and is at its best when the inside is slightly pink whilst there is a brown crust on the outside.

Grilled heart

1 beef heart, cut into ½ inch-   ¼ pint dry red wine
   thick slices   1 clove garlic (crushed)
¼ pint olive oil   salt and black pepper to taste
3 tablespoons vinegar

Mix together olive oil, vinegar, wine, garlic, salt and pepper. Marinate the heart in this mixture for 3–4 hours, or overnight, turning several times. Drain well.

Barbecue over medium coals, with the grill set about 4 inches from coals, giving each side approximately 3–4 minutes. Baste frequently with the marinade. The heart will be done when centre is a light pink colour. Do not overcook as the meat will quickly become tough.

Spiced chicken   Serves 4

1 chicken (about 3 lb), quartered	$\frac{1}{8}$ teaspoon cinnamon
3 oz butter	$\frac{1}{2}$ teaspoon salt
$\frac{1}{4}$ teaspoon paprika	1 clove garlic, crushed
	$\frac{1}{8}$ teaspoon crushed tarragon

Wash the chicken quarters and pat dry with paper towelling. Melt the butter and blend with the paprika, cinnamon, salt, garlic and tarragon.

Barbecue the chicken quarters over medium coals, brushing frequently with the butter mixture, and turning occasionally. The chicken should be well browned and tender after about 40 minutes on the grill.

When barbecuing chicken halves and quarters, breaking the wing and knee joints will help to keep the meat flat on the grill.

Lemon-basted chicken   Serves 4

1 2$\frac{1}{2}$–3 lb chicken cut into serving pieces

Lemon basting sauce

3 oz butter	1 teaspoon salt
2 tablespoons lemon juice	$\frac{1}{4}$ teaspoon white pepper
$\frac{1}{2}$ teaspoon garlic juice	$\frac{1}{2}$ teaspoon paprika

Wash the chicken pieces and pat dry with paper towels. Melt the butter and blend with lemon juice, garlic juice, salt, pepper and paprika.

Place the chicken pieces on the barbecue grill over medium

coals, brush occasionally with the basting sauce, turning every few minutes until the chicken is well browned and tender. It will take about 35–40 minutes.

Turkey drumsticks   Serves 4

4 turkey drumsticks   ¼ pint sour cream

Marinade
6 tablespoons dry red wine   1½ teaspoons chili powder
½ pint salad oil   ¼ teaspoon pepper
½ teaspoon crushed dried   ¼ teaspoon seasoned salt
  oregano   2 tablespoons brown sugar
¼ teaspoon garlic powder

Combine all the marinade ingredients and mix together thoroughly. Marinate the drumsticks in a refrigerator for about one hour, turning once during that time. After removing drumsticks, place the marinade in a small pot and heat (do not allow to boil).

Place the drumsticks on a greased grill, set about 6 inches above medium coals, and cover with the lid of the barbecue, or alternatively with a tent made from heavy-duty aluminium foil (details are given on p. 32 on how to make a cover from foil). The drumsticks should be turned and basted occasionally with the warmed marinade, during a cooking time of approximately 1½ hours (2 hours if the barbecue is uncovered). If you have one, insert a meat thermometer into the thickest part of a drumstick after an hour's cooking. Continue cooking until the temperature reaches 185°F. The turkey is done when the meat is tender and no red juices appear when the flesh is pierced.

Some of the remaining marinade can be used to make a sauce, a few minutes before taking the drumsticks off the grill. Gradually blend 3 tablespoons of the marinade into ¼ pint of sour cream. Heat the mixture slowly until just heated through – do not bring to boiling point. Transfer the sauce to a pre-heated bowl and serve at once.

Grilled meat tarts with mushroom filling   Serves 6

1½ lb minced lean beef	1 tablespoon finely chopped
3 tablespoons dry	onion
breadcrumbs (rubbed fine)	2 tablespoons butter or
½ teaspoon salt	margarine
¼ teaspoon black pepper	3 oz grated Cheddar cheese
1 egg	6 aluminium-foil individual
½ lb mushrooms, quartered	tart moulds

Place the minced beef, breadcrumbs, salt, pepper and egg in a bowl and blend. Divide the mixture into six equal portions and form each portion into a ½-inch-thick patty about 4 inches in diameter. Press each patty into a foil mould, covering the bottom and sides of the mould.

Place them upside down on the grill and cook over medium coals until the meat starts to turn brown. Take care not to overcook the meat or it will become dry. With care the meat should come away quite easily from the foil mould.

Whilst the meat is cooking, sauté the mushrooms and onion in the butter in a small pan. Add a pinch of salt and pepper. When the mushrooms are cooked, use them to fill the meat shells and then top each one with grated cheese. Put them on the grill again and cook until the cheese melts.

Minced beef loaf   Serves 4

1½ lb minced lean beef	1 teaspoon salt
2 oz butter or margarine	¼ teaspoon black pepper

Lemon–butter sauce

1 oz butter or margarine	pinch of salt
pinch of paprika	pinch of pepper
1 tablespoon lemon juice	1 teaspoon chopped parsley

Season the meat with salt and pepper and form the mixture into a small loaf about 1½ inches thick and 3 inches wide. Spread the butter or margarine over the loaf.

Before barbecuing the meat, prepare the lemon–butter sauce by melting the butter and adding salt, pepper, paprika, lemon juice and parsley. Stir well and when the sauce is well blended, set it to one side.

With the grill set low (about 2–3 inches above the coals) cook each side of the loaf for about 6 minutes. Carefully turn the meat by using a wide-bladed spatula. As soon as the loaf is cooked, cut it into four portions and pour the lemon–butter sauce over it.

After cooking for the prescribed period, the loaf should appear brown and crusty on the outside and be somewhat rare in its centre.

Aloha mince–steaks Serves 6

1 lb minced lamb or lean beef	9-oz can pineapple slices
dash of pepper	2 oz brown sugar
¼ teaspoon salt	2 tsps Worcestershire sauce
1 teaspoon soy sauce	6 tablespoons tomato sauce

Place the minced meat, salt, pepper and soy sauce in a bowl and mix well. Shape into six patties.

Drain the pineapple, retaining about 2 tablespoons of juice. Press a pineapple slice into the surface of each patty and mould the meat around the edges of slice to hold it firmly during cooking.

Place the sugar, Worcestershire sauce, pineapple juice and

tomato sauce in a pan and heat gently for a few minutes. Brush the sauce over the patties and grill over hot coals for about 10 minutes, or until meat is done and the pineapple is glazed.

Brush the patties frequently with sauce during the cooking period.

Basic hamburgers   Serves 6

1½ lb good-quality minced beef	pinch of freshly ground pepper
1 onion, finely minced	6 soft rolls
3 teaspoons salt	

Mix beef and onion together, season well and shape into six hamburgers approximately ½ inch thick. Barbecue over hot coals for about 10 minutes each side – turning once. The hamburgers can be basted during cooking with one of the suitable sauces, or marinades, listed in Chapter 12. Serve in rolls, which should be toasted on the barbecue grill during the final few minutes of the hamburgers' cooking.

Chuck wagon hamburgers   Serves 8

1 lb finely minced chuck steak	1 clove garlic, crushed
1 green pepper, finely chopped	1½ tablespoons cooking oil
	pinch salt
1 small onion, finely chopped	¼ teaspoon freshly ground pepper
2 medium carrots, grated	1 egg
2 sticks celery, finely chopped	8 soft rolls
2 teaspoons Worcestershire sauce	8 slices tomato

Lightly mix together the minced steak, green pepper, onion, carrots, celery, Worcestershire sauce, garlic, oil, salt and pepper, and bind with the egg. Shape into eight equal-size patties and cook on the grill, over hot coals, for approximately 10 minutes each side. Toast the rolls as the hamburgers finish cooking. Place a tomato slice on each hamburger and serve in the buttered rolls.

Cheddar-cheese burgers   Serves 6

1½ lb finely minced lean beef
¾ teaspoon salt
pinch freshly ground pepper

6 thin slices Cheddar cheese
6 soft rolls

Lightly mix together the minced beef, salt and pepper and shape into six patties. Cook the first side over hot coals for approximately 8–10 minutes or until meat is nicely browned. Shortly after turning the patties over, top with the cheese slices and continue cooking until cheese starts to melt. During the last few minutes of cooking toast the rolls on the grill. Serve the cheese burgers in the rolls.

Cheese and bacon burgers   Serves 6

1½ lb finely minced chuck
   steak
¾ teaspoon salt
pinch freshly ground pepper
   (optional)

4 tablespoons grated Cheddar
   cheese
3 rashers bacon (streaky or
   short back)
6 soft rolls

Lightly mix together the minced beef, salt and pepper. Shape into six patties and cook over hot coals for approximately 8–10 minutes. Shortly after turning, sprinkle the grated cheese on the patties and start grilling the bacon rashers. When crisp the rashers should be diced and scattered over the melting cheese. Toast the rolls as usual during the last few minutes, and serve.

Red wine hamburgers   Serves 6–8

1½ lb finely minced beef
5 tablespoons dry red wine
2 oz butter or margarine
2 medium-size onions, finely chopped
1½ oz fine breadcrumbs (from fresh white bread)
1 teaspoon salt
¼ teaspoon freshly ground pepper (optional)
1 large egg
soft rolls

Put half of the red wine, butter and chopped onion to one side. Lightly mix the remaining ingredients and shape into six to eight hamburgers, approximately ¾-inch thick. Melt the butter or margarine in a saucepan, add the remainder of the chopped onion and sauté until yellow and transparent. Add the remaining wine and simmer for approximately 5 minutes.

Brush the wine and onion sauce over the hamburgers and cook over hot coals for about 8–10 minutes each side. Brush the sauce on the hamburgers occasionally during cooking. Toast the rolls, and serve.

Hot soy hamburgers   Serves 4

1 lb finely minced chuck steak
1 small onion, finely chopped
¼ teaspoon dry mustard
2 teaspoons soy sauce
1½ tablespoons chili sauce
2 teaspoons horseradish sauce
4 soft rolls

Lightly mix all the ingredients with a fork and shape into four hamburgers. Cook on the grill over hot coals for approximately 10 minutes each side, or until nicely browned. Toast the rolls, and serve.

Hamburgers with spicy sauce   Serves 8

2¼ lb lean raw minced beef
1 teaspoon salt
½ teaspoon pepper

1 medium-size onion, finely
  chopped

Sauce
2 tablespoons Worcestershire
  sauce
4 tablespoons tomato ketchup
½ teaspoon prepared English
  mustard

1 tablespoon clear honey
2 teaspoons lemon juice
2 tablespoons water

Combine all the hamburger ingredients and mix together thoroughly, using a fork. Shape into eight hamburgers. Combine all the sauce ingredients in a pan and heat, stirring well.

Place the hamburgers on a greased grill about 5 inches above medium coals, and brush generously with the sauce. Cook about 4 minutes each side if preferred rare, and 6–8 minutes for medium done. Heat the remaining sauce and serve with the hamburgers.

Basic hot dog   Serves 6

6 frankfurters
6 long rolls

butter

Place frankfurters on the grill and cook for 6–10 minutes, turning frequently, over medium coals. During the last minute or so of cooking, toast the split rolls. Butter the toasted rolls, fill with the frankfurters and garnish with mustard, onions or a sauce.

Frankfurter and pineapple

Slit open each frankfurter along its length and place a strip of pineapple in the opening. Wrap a rasher of streaky bacon around the frankfurter and secure with wooden cocktail sticks. Grill until the bacon is crisp on all sides. Remove sticks before serving.

Cheese dogs

Slit open each frankfurter along its length and lay in a long wedge-shaped piece of Cheddar cheese. Cook, with the cheese uppermost, until the frankfurter is hot and the cheese melted.

Frankfurter kebabs

Cut each frankfurter into three pieces and alternate on skewers with pineapple chunks and slices of small onions (optional). Grill over medium coals until frankfurter pieces are well browned. Serve in buttered toasted rolls or as an appetizer.

Smoke-cooked chicken   Serves 4

1 frying chicken (2–3 lb)	hickory or green apple-wood
3 rashers smoked streaky	chips
bacon	

The chicken should be cooked in a barbecue that has a cover or lid, i.e. a kettle or wagon grill. Alternatively, a loose covering of heavy-duty aluminium foil will help to contain the smoke (details on how to make an aluminium-foil cover are given on p. 32).

Shortly after setting light to the charcoal, place a handful of hickory, or apple-wood, chips in a bowl of water.

Place the chicken on a greased grill, set about 6 inches above a bed of hot coals. Lay the bacon rashers on top of the chicken.

A few minutes after the chicken starts cooking, position a few wood chips, using tongs, on top of the coals. The amount of smoke, and therefore smoke flavour, produced is determined by the number of chips added during barbecuing. Do not add too many chips at any one time. As soon as the chicken becomes well browned on one side, it should be turned over and the bacon re-positioned. The chicken should be ready in about $1\frac{1}{4}$ hours and covered by a glaze formed from the smoke-laden bacon fat.

Boned leg of lamb with mushrooms   Serves 8–10

1 boned and rolled leg of lamb (5–6 lb)	$\frac{1}{4}$ teaspoon oregano
	$\frac{1}{4}$ teaspoon thyme
8 large mushrooms (about 3 inches in diameter)	1 teaspoon salt
	$\frac{1}{4}$ teaspoon pepper
$\frac{1}{2}$ pint olive oil	6 oz finely chopped onion
8 tablespoons dry red wine	3 oz butter

Remove the stems from the mushrooms and scrape some of the fronds from the centre of the hollow. Put the stems and mushroom pieces to one side.

Marinate the lamb and mushroom caps overnight in a mixture of the olive oil, red wine, oregano, thyme, salt and pepper.

Finely chop all the mushroom stems and pieces and combine with the onion. Melt the butter, add the mixture of onion and mushroom and cook until tender. Season to taste with salt and pepper and set aside. Barbecue the meat over medium to hot coals, for about 50 minutes. The meat should be turned frequently during cooking and occasionally basted with the marinade. Remove the mushroom caps from the marinade about

15–20 minutes before the meat is done. Having drained the caps, place them, hollow side down, on the grill and cook for 4–5 minutes. Turn the caps over and spoon the onion-mushroom mixture into the hollows. Cook the caps for another 10 minutes or so, basting once or twice during this period with the marinade.

The lamb should be carved by slicing across the grain.

Spit-roasted leg of lamb   Serves 8–10

1 leg of lamb (5–6 lb)	½ teaspoon crushed dried
4 cloves garlic, sliced	oregano
1 teaspoon salt	4 tablespoons melted butter
	juice of one small lemon

Slit the surface of the meat in several places and insert slivers of garlic and a mixture of the salt and oregano. Rub the outside of the meat with any remaining salt and oregano mixture. Insert the spit almost parallel to the bone and place over medium coals.

Mix the melted butter and lemon juice and use to baste the meat a couple of times during the cooking period. The meat is at its best when still slightly pink in the centre (medium rare) and it should take about 1¼–1½ hours. The temperature reading on a meat thermometer will be 140–150°F.

Glazed shoulder of lamb   Serves 7–10

3–4 lb shoulder of lamb,	garlic clove (optional)
boned and rolled	½ pint redcurrant jelly
salt and pepper	2 teaspoons prepared mustard

Rub the meat with salt and pepper. Slit the surface in several places and insert slivers of garlic. Secure the shoulder on the spit. Cook the meat over medium coals, allowing 25–30 minutes per pound, or until a meat thermometer reads 180°F. Place a drip pan made from aluminium foil (see p. 29) under the meat. During the last 30 minutes of cooking time, baste the lamb shoulder with a glaze made by melting the currant jelly and stirring in the mustard.

Marinated pork on the spit   Serves 6–8

1 leg of pork, boned (allow
  about 6–8 oz per person)
1 pint cider
4 tablespoons lemon juice
4 tablespoons orange juice

4 tablespoons vinegar
½ teaspoon garlic salt
½ teaspoon onion salt
¼ teaspoon black pepper or
  cayenne pepper

Mix together all the seasoning ingredients and use to marinate the pork overnight. After draining, score the leg evenly and mount on the spit. Brush the meat well with the marinade and cook slowly over medium coals, allowing about 25 minutes per pound. Place a drip pan under the meat to catch the juices, and use them to make gravy.

During cooking, brush the meat frequently with the marinade.

11 Shish-kebabs

Shish-kebab, kabobs or simply kebabs – the name may vary but it all adds up to the technique of cooking food on a skewer (usually metal, but slivers of bamboo are used in the Orient).

Broadly speaking, there is virtually no limit to the combination of ingredients that can be grilled shish-kebab style. Lamb, beef, poultry, veal, pork, ham, cocktail sausages, chicken livers, bacon and a variety of seafood are particularly suitable. Cheaper and coarser cuts of meat are best marinated (see Chapter 12 for marinade recipes) before cooking. In addition to meat and fish there are several vegetables and fruit which can be skewer cooked such as pineapple chunks, small

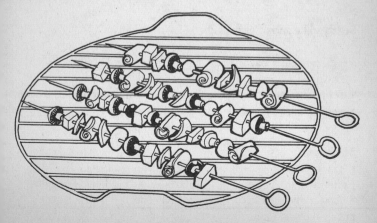

tomatoes, small whole onions, green pepper pieces, apple quarters, firm peach quarters, olives, orange segments, corn-on-the-cob (two-inch pieces) and water chestnuts. When cooking vegetables and meats on the same skewer, the meat pieces should be smaller than the vegetables to ensure that everything will be ready to eat at the same time. It may be more practical, when cooking for more than six people, to use separate skewers for the meat and vegetables in order to control the cooking period more precisely.

Some people might enjoy preparing, and then cooking their own kebabs (memories perhaps of bygone Scout and Guide camps) so don't be afraid of allowing your guests to make up their own shish-kebab skewers from bowls of pre-pared ingredients. If you decide to let your guests 'do it themselves' remember to have an adequate number of mitts available, if the skewers are without hardwood handles, as the skewer is likely to become very hot.

Mechanically turned skewers are available but hand skewers are the most commonly used and during the cooking period these have to be constantly turned in order to cook the food evenly and prevent charring.

Seafood kebabs   Serves 4

6 rashers streaky bacon (rind removed)
8 oz plaice fillets
3 crayfish tails, peeled

8 large cooked prawns, peeled
1 large lemon cut into four thick slices
salt and pepper

Marinade
1 lemon
¼ pint olive oil
1 clove garlic, crushed

¼ teaspoon salt
freshly ground black pepper
1 bay leaf

Seafood sauce

6 tablespoons thick
mayonnaise
1 tablespoon tomato purée
2 tablespoons lemon juice
1 tablespoon Worcestershire
sauce

1 teaspoon grated lemon rind
1 teaspoon finely chopped
onion
2 teaspoons chopped parsley
salt and freshly ground black
pepper

Prepare the marinade by carefully paring the rind from the lemon. Add the rind to the juice squeezed from the lemon, oil, garlic, salt, pepper and bay leaf and mix together thoroughly. Place the bacon rashers on a board and stretch with the back of a round-bladed knife. Cut each in two. Remove the skin from the plaice fillets and divide into twelve pieces. Place each piece on a rasher of bacon, season and roll up, enclosing the fish. Secure each with a cocktail stick. Cut each crayfish tail into four equal pieces. Place the bacon rolls, prawns and crayfish in the marinade and leave for 4 hours in a cool place, turning occasionally. Meanwhile prepare the sauce. Stir all the ingredients together and season to taste. Leave for at least 4 hours before serving.

Remove the seafood from marinade and strain the marinade. Cut each lemon slice into four pieces. Remove the cocktail sticks from the bacon rolls and put them with the prawns and crayfish on four long or eight shorter skewers alternating with pieces of lemon.

Place the skewers on an oiled grill and cook for 8–10 minutes, or until fish is done, turning and brushing occasionally with the marinade.

Serve with the sauce.

Variation

Other seafood such as scallops and lobster can be used, cut if necessary, into appropriate-sized pieces.

Prawn kebabs   Serves 4–6

1½ lb fresh pawns (or very large shrimps)
2 tablespoons melted butter (or margarine)
¾ tablespoon lemon juice
½ teaspoon salt

pinch of pepper
¼ lb button mushrooms
5 slices lean bacon cut into squares
1 lemon – sliced

Peel the prawns and de-vein if desired. Rinse well and pat dry with paper towel.

Combine the butter, lemon juice, salt and pepper and mix well. Alternate prawns, mushrooms and bacon squares on skewers and brush with the seasoned butter.

Cook with the grill set about 4–5 inches above hot coals. After 5 minutes cooking turn the kebabs over, brush with more butter and continue cooking for another 3–5 minutes.

Serve with lemon slices.

Lobster and steak kebabs   Serves 4–6

1 large lobster
1 lb sirloin or rump steak cut into 1½-inch cubes
2 green peppers, cut in pieces

3 tablespoons Sauternes
3 tablespoons lemon juice
3 tablespoons salad oil

The lobster should be killed and cleaned just before cooking (see instructions on p. 87).

Take the white meat from the lobster and cut into 1½-inch pieces. Alternate the lobster, steak and green-pepper pieces on skewers. Cook with the grill set about 4–5 inches above hot coals. Combine the wine, lemon juice and salad oil and use to baste the kebabs during the cooking period, approximately 12–15 minutes.

Ginger teriyaki   Serves 6

2 lb sirloin steak cut into
   ¼-inch-thick slices
4 fluid ounces soy sauce
1 tablespoon ground ginger

2 fluid ounces sake or sherry
1 minced garlic clove
sugar

Mix together soy sauce, ginger, sake or sherry, garlic and sugar (1 teaspoon to 3 tablespoons according to taste). Marinade the steak in this mixture for approximately one hour. Drain well. Weave meat on to skewers – using one skewer for each strip of meat. Barbecue over hot coals, 1–2 minutes only each side, basting with the marinade.

Veal saté   Serves 6

2 lb boneless veal leg or
   shoulder, cut into one-inch
   cubes

Marinade
¾ tablespoon salt
4 oz chopped onion
1 tablespoon ground
   coriander
½ teaspoon ground pepper
3 tablespoons lemon juice
6 tablespoons soy sauce

6 tablespoons peanut butter
6 tablespoons groundnut or
   salad oil
2 oz brown sugar
2 cloves garlic
pinch of cayenne

Place all the marinade ingredients in a liquidizer and blend to a smooth consistency. Marinate the meat in the mixture for about 2 hours.

   Impale the meat on skewers and barbecue over hot coals. Each side should be given about 3 minutes cooking and the meat should be browned but not dry. Serve with the remaining marinade.

Variation

Replace veal with boned chicken.

Spiced pork saté   Serves 6

2 lb boneless pork loin	3 tablespoons tomato sauce
6 tablespoons chutney	½ teaspoon chili powder
1 tablespoon soy sauce	Indonesian sauce (p. 137)
2 tablespoons salad oil	

Finely chop the chutney (or purée in a blender). Place it in a mixing bowl and add the soy sauce, chili powder, tomato sauce and salad oil. Cut the meat into one-inch squares (about ¾-inch thick) and marinate in the mixture for about 4 hours, turning occasionally.

Impale the meat pieces on six skewers, or bamboo sticks, and barbecue over hot coals for about 12 minutes, ensuring that all sides of the meat are browned.

Reheat the Indonesian sauce gently and serve with the saté.

Spicy lamb kebabs   Serves 4

1½ lb leg of lamb, top end	8 shallots or 2 medium onions
1 green pepper	8 button mushrooms

Marinade

¼ pint Worcestershire sauce	1 onion, finely chopped
4 tablespoons water	2 teaspoons sugar
2 tablespoons oil	1 teaspoon salt

Combine all the marinade ingredients in a pan, bring to the boil, cover and simmer for 10 minutes. Allow to cool.

Cut the lamb into one-inch cubes, removing any fat. Place the meat cubes in a bowl and pour the marinade over them. Leave at room temperature for about 4 hours or keep overnight in a refrigerator, turning the meat over once or twice. Cut the pepper in half, remove the seeds and cut each half into four. Parboil the shallots or onions. If medium-sized onions are used cut each onion into four.

Arrange the lamb cubes on four skewers alternately with the vegetables. Brush with the marinade and place on an oiled grill about 4 inches above hot coals. Turn frequently and baste with the remaining marinade. Barbecue for about 15 minutes until all sides are browned.

Serve with rice, boiled with a pinch of turmeric, and with tomato sauce.

Pineapple and lamb kebabs   Serves 4

1 lb lean lamb, cut into 1½-inch cubes	3 tablespoons honey
8 small tomatoes	2 tablespoons melted butter
15-oz can pineapple chunks (save syrup)	1 clove garlic, crushed
8 oz small mushrooms	1 teaspoon Worcestershire sauce
1 green pepper, cut in small pieces	1 teaspoon salt
3 tablespoons vinegar	¼ teaspoon pepper
	¼ teaspoon ginger powder

Alternate the lamb cubes with tomatoes, pineapple chunks, mushrooms and peppers on skewers. Add the pineapple syrup to the remaining ingredients and mix well. Brush kebabs with the mixture and cook about 4–5 inches above medium coals for 15–20 minutes, basting and turning occasionally.

Lamb kidney brochette with sauce Bercy   Serves 4–6

12 lamb kidneys	3 tablespoons melted butter

Sauce Bercy

1 tablespoon minced shallots	2 teaspoons flour
3 oz butter	1 tablespoon minced parsley
½ pint dry white wine	salt and pepper

Remove the fat and skin from the kidneys and split each kidney, from the inside edge, to within half an inch of the outer surface. Extract the white membrane from the inside. Thread on fine skewers, using a wide stitch across the back of the kidney to hold it in an open position.

Brush the kidneys with melted butter and grill over hot coals, basting occasionally with butter, for about 3 minutes each side. Do not be tempted to overcook as the kidneys will rapidly become tough.

Shortly before starting to cook the kidneys, prepare the sauce Bercy. Place the minced shallots and 1 oz of butter in a saucepan and cook until soft. Add the wine and simmer until the liquid has reduced to about half. Mix together the remaining butter and flour and add to the liquid in pan. Continue cooking and stirring until the mixture thickens. Stir in the minced parsley and add salt and pepper to taste.

Sausage and kidney kebabs   Serves 4

6 oz streaky bacon, rind removed	4 lamb's kidneys, skinned, halved, core removed
4 skinless sausages, cut in half	4 small tomatoes

Baste

1 teaspoon tomato purée	1 tablespoon oil
1 teaspoon Worcestershire sauce	

Stretch bacon rashers on a board with the back of a round-bladed knife and cut in half. Roll up each piece and secure on four skewers, alternating with sausages, kidneys and tomatoes. Combine the basting ingredients and brush over the kebabs. Place on oiled grill over medium coals and cook for 5 minutes on each side. Continue to baste during cooking.

Sweetbread and steak kebabs   Serves 4–6

1 lb rump steak, cut ¾-inch
   thick, in one-inch squares
1 lb sweetbreads
1 tablespoon lemon juice
1 teaspoon salt

2 rashers of lean bacon
6 fresh mushrooms
   (1–2 inches in diameter)
tarragon butter (see p. 140)

Wash the sweetbreads thoroughly in cold water and then allow to soak for about 3 hours, changing the water once or twice every hour. Drain and cover the sweetbreads with about 2½ pints of cold water (just sufficient to cover them). Add the lemon juice and salt. Bring rapidly to the boil and then simmer for 15 minutes. Drain and then immerse the sweetbreads in cold water for a few minutes. After draining again, remove as much of the white membrane as possible (a small sharp knife will help here). Cut the sweetbreads into pieces about the same size as the steak squares.

Partially cook the bacon rashers on the grill, remove and cut into one-inch pieces. Alternate steak, bacon and sweetbread pieces on six skewers and place a mushroom cap on the end of each skewer. Cook, with the grill set about 4–5 inches above medium coals, for approximately 12 minutes and turn frequently to ensure even cooking. During the grilling period brush the kebabs several times with the tarragon butter. Serve the remainder with the kebabs.

Sweetbread and mushroom kebabs   Serves 4–6

1½ lb lamb sweetbreads	1 oz soft white breadcrumbs
2 tablespoons salt	¼ lb melted butter
2 tablespoons vinegar	12 mushrooms

Soak the sweetbreads for at least an hour in cold water. Drain and put in a pan adding 2 quarts of water, vinegar and salt. Bring slowly to the boil and simmer for about 10–15 minutes. Drain and plunge into cold water.

Remove any gristle and skin and cut the sweetbreads into 1½-inch pieces. Dip them in the melted butter and dust with breadcrumbs. Impale the pieces on skewers with mushrooms in between and place on an oiled grill about 3 inches above medium coals. Turn the skewers every few minutes and brush with softened butter. The sweetbreads will be done when evenly browned.

Chicken liver and pork kebabs   Serves 4–6

1 lb lean pork sliced ½ inch thick	4 tablespoons chicken stock
1 lb chicken livers	3 tablespoons dry sherry or apple juice
6 tablespoons soy sauce	1½ tablespoons brown sugar
2 tablespoons melted butter or bacon dripping	pinch of salt

Cut the pork slices into pieces about 1½-inches square. Alternate the pork pieces with chicken livers on skewers. Combine the remaining ingredients and mix well. Marinate the kebabs in the mixture for 1–2 hours, turning often.

Cook with the grill set about 4–5 inches above hot coals. The kebabs should be turned frequently and basted with the marinade. Cook for about 20–25 minutes.

Spiced ox liver kebabs   Serves 4–6

2 lb ox liver, sliced $\frac{1}{2}$ inch thick

Marinade

$\frac{1}{4}$ pint olive oil

1 oz chopped fresh mint

1 tablespoon lemon juice

2 teaspoons salt

1 clove garlic, crushed

pinch of freshly ground
   black pepper

2 tablespoons olive oil

Combine the marinade ingredients except the 2 tablespoons olive oil, and spread the mixture on both sides of the liver. Allow to stand for about 3 hours. Cut the liver into 2-inch squares and thread on two skewers to keep the meat flat. Barbecue the kebabs quickly over hot coals allowing about 2 minutes for each side. Baste frequently with the remaining marinade to which you have added the 2 tablespoons of olive oil. Do not overcook the liver which, when ready, should be pink, and slightly juicy inside.

Bacon kebabs   Serves 4

$1\frac{1}{4}$ lb shoulder bacon joint,
   cut into one-inch cubes

8 button onions

1 large green pepper, seeds
   removed, blanched and
   cut into one-inch squares

12 button mushrooms

Marinade

1 tablespoon oil

2 tablespoons Worcestershire
   sauce

grated rind and juice of a
   large orange

salt and pepper

Combine all the marinade ingredients in a shallow dish. Place the bacon cubes in the marinade and leave for 2 hours, turning occasionally. Cook the onions in boiling water for 5 minutes.

Drain the bacon, reserving the marinade, and thread on to 4 skewers, alternating with the pepper, onions and mushrooms. Brush the kebabs with the marinade and place on an oiled grill about 4 inches above medium coals. Barbecue for 12–15 minutes, turning frequently.

Heart kebabs   Serves 4–6

1 beef heart (approximately 3 lb)
$\frac{1}{2}$ teaspoon ground pepper
1$\frac{1}{2}$ teaspoons chili powder
3 tablespoons water
1$\frac{1}{2}$ teaspoons salt
6 tablespoons vinegar
2 cloves garlic – crushed
6 tablespoons olive oil

Remove hard fat and tubes from heart. Cut into one-inch cubes. Combine chili powder, salt, garlic, pepper, water, vinegar and olive oil and marinate the beef cubes in the mixture overnight. Position cubes well apart on the skewers and grill over hot coals for about 2–3 minutes on each side of cube (approximately 8–12 minutes total cooking time). Baste each side of cube once with the marinade.

Do not overcook otherwise the beef heart will become tough.

12 Marinades, sauces and flavoured butters

Marinades and basting sauces play an important part in the successful preparation of certain meats. Marinades are used primarily to tenderize and enhance the flavour of the meat. They also help to impart moistness to very lean meats. The acid in a marinade (wine, vinegar or citrus juice) acts as a tenderizing agent; the fat (melted butter, margarine or oil) keeps lean meats moist and thus helps to prevent the meat from drying out when being cooked over hot coals. As a general rule use oily marinades on dry or lean foods and non-oily marinades (wine or vinegar based) on foods with a high fat content.

To marinate meat, cover it with the prepared mixture and chill in a refrigerator for several hours (the recipe will state how long the food should be kept in the marinade). Turn it several times to allow the flavour to penetrate more evenly. Take the food out of the marinade, drain off the excess liquid, and allow the meat, etc, to come to room temperature before barbecuing – otherwise the cooking period required will be more difficult to judge. The leftover marinade can either be stored for future use (it should be kept in an airtight container in the refrigerator) or used as a baste whilst the meat is cooking.

Cooking sauces are brushed, or spooned, over the meat, poultry or seafood whilst they are being cooked and often the word 'sauce' is used in the same context as 'marinade' or 'baste'. A cooking sauce should contain melted butter, margarine or oil to keep the meat moist and various seasonings to impart flavour.

Sauces can be kept in fireproof containers and placed in a convenient position next to the grill (it is possible to buy a cheap clip-on shelf to suit most barbecues).

A basic barbecue marinade

3 tablespoons dry sherry
2 tablespoons soy sauce
3 tablespoons salad oil
1 teaspoon Worcestershire
  sauce

1 teaspoon garlic powder
freshly ground black pepper
  to taste

This marinade can be used for meat, poultry or fish. Combine sherry, soy sauce, salad oil, Worcestershire sauce, garlic powder and pepper. Pour the marinade over the food and leave in the refrigerator (turning occasionally) for a varying period of time according to the type of food: steaks will need 3–5 hours (depending upon thickness), roasts 24–48 hours (depending upon roast size), poultry 2 hours, salmon 2 hours.

This marinade can also be used as a basting sauce.

Soy rum marinade

3 tablespoons soy sauce
6 tablespoons light rum
3 tablespoons pineapple juice
¾ tablespoon brown sugar
  (packed tightly)

1 teaspoon garlic salt
1 teaspoon dry mustard
½ teaspoon pepper
2 teaspoons ground ginger

Combine all the ingredients in a saucepan and simmer for approximately 5–6 minutes. When the marinade has cooled use to marinate chicken pieces.

Honey-orange marinade

6 tablespoons honey
6 tablespoons soy sauce
½ pint orange juice
3 tablespoons water
1½ pint dry white wine
1 teaspoon dry mustard
1 teaspoon paprika
¼ teaspoon allspice
1 clove garlic, crushed
dash of tabasco sauce
  (optional)

Combine all the ingredients well. Let the marinade stand for about one hour before using to marinate spareribs, chicken or ham. The remaining marinade should be used to baste the meat during barbecuing.

Seafare marinade

¼ pint dry white wine
3 tablespoons oil
1 teaspoon paprika
½ teaspoon salt
⅛ teaspoon pepper
1 teaspoon sugar
¾ tablespoon minced parsley

Combine all the ingredients and pour over seafood. There should be sufficient marinade for approximately 2 lb.

Teriyaki marinade

1½ tablespoons honey (or
  2 tablespoons brown sugar)
1½ tablespoons salad oil
4 tablespoons soy sauce
¾ tablespoon dry red wine
  (or red wine vinegar)
1 teaspoon freshly grated
  ginger (or ⅕ teaspoon
  ginger powder)
1 clove garlic, crushed

Use for poultry, beef, spareribs and fish, and also as a basting sauce.

Combine all the ingredients. Pour marinade over food and leave in the refrigerator (turning occasionally) for varying periods of time to suit the type of food. Chicken or spareribs should be marinated for 4–8 hours; beef for 8 hours; fish for 2–4 hours.

Honey marinade for lamb

½ pint dry white wine
1½ tablespoons wine vinegar
2 cloves garlic, crushed
1 teaspoon salt

1½ tablespoons salad oil or melted butter
4 tablespoons honey
1 teaspoon chopped mint

Combine all the ingredients, place in a saucepan and heat until the marinade is simmering. Remove from heat and cover. Let the marinade stand for about an hour and then pour over the lamb chops, breast, steaks or shank. Marinate for 1–4 hours, depending upon how strongly you want the marinade flavour to permeate the lamb. The remaining marinade is good for basting the lamb whilst barbecuing.

Wine marinade for chicken

½ pint dry white wine
3 tablespoons lemon juice
1½ tablespoons wine vinegar
2 cloves garlic, crushed

1 teaspoon dried whole tarragon or rosemary
1 teaspoon salt
1½ tablespoons melted butter or salad oil

Combine all the ingredients in a saucepan and heat until the marinade is simmering. Remove from heat and cover the saucepan. Let the marinade stand for about an hour and then pour over the chicken pieces. Marinate for 1–4 hours, depending upon how strongly you want the marinade flavour to penetrate the chicken. Use the leftover marinade as a basting sauce during barbecuing.

Red wine marinade

½ pint dry red wine
1 teaspoon dried whole basil
or oregano
2 cloves garlic, crushed

1 teaspoon salt
2 tablespoons wine vinegar
1½ tablespoons melted butter
or salad oil

This is good for pork or beef. Combine all the ingredients and heat in a saucepan until the marinade starts to simmer. Remove immediately from the heat, cover the pan and allow to stand for about an hour. Pour over the meat (steak, spareribs or pork chops) and marinate for 2–5 hours, according to taste.

Mint marinade

1½ tablespoons mint leaves
(minced)
½ pint dry white wine
4 tablespoons olive oil
1 clove garlic, crushed
¼ teaspoon freshly ground
black pepper

¼ teaspoon crushed basil
¾ tablespoon minced parsley
(fresh or dried)
½ teaspoon salt
1 teaspoon sugar

Combine all the ingredients well. These quantities will make about ½ pint of marinade. Use to marinate lamb or chicken; pour the marinade over the meat and leave for 2–3 hours.

Western-style barbecue sauce

3 tablespoons Worcestershire
  sauce
1 teaspoon chili powder
1 teaspoon dry mustard
1 teaspoon salt
1 teaspoon freshly ground
  pepper
4 tablespoons honey

½ pint chili sauce
½ pint tomato sauce
2 dashes Tabasco sauce
3 tablespoons wine vinegar
6 tablespoons water
3 tablespoons tarragon
  vinegar

This sauce is particularly good for basting ribs during the last
few minutes of barbecuing. Mix all the ingredients together,
and add a little more water if it is too thick.

Sweet and sour sauce

¼ pint dry white wine
1½ tablespoons white wine
  vinegar
1½ tablespoons salad oil
½ pint crushed pineapple
  (undrained)
1 tablespoon soy sauce

1 teaspoon lemon juice
¼ teaspoon garlic salt
½ teaspoon dry mustard
1½ tablespoons brown sugar
¾ tablespoon chopped onion
  (optional)

Combine all the ingredients – mixing well – and simmer in a
saucepan for about 10–15 minutes. Use to baste poultry, pork,
lamb, ribs and fish steaks.

Tomato chili sauce

1 large onion, finely chopped
2 tablespoons oil

14-oz can tomatoes
1 tablespoon tomato purée

2 teaspoons chili seasoning
1 tablespoon Worcestershire
  sauce
¼ pint chicken stock

½ teaspoon salt
2 teaspoons cornflour
2 tablespoons water

Cook the onion gently in oil until soft. Add all remaining ingredients except the cornflour and water. Bring to the boil, cover and cook gently for 15 minutes. Sieve or liquidize. Return to the saucepan and mix in the cornflour blended with the water. Bring to boil, again stirring all the time, and cook until thickened. Adjust seasoning.

Use as a dunking sauce for chicken drumsticks or spoon a little sauce over drumsticks when they are taken off the barbecue.

Horseradish sauce   Serves 4–6

¼ pint double cream
1 tablespoon lemon juice
1 teaspoon horseradish sauce

2 teaspoons Worcestershire
  sauce
2 spring onions, finely
  chopped

Mix together double cream and lemon juice. Blend in remaining ingredients. Allow to stand for at least 4 hours before serving. Serve with barbecued steaks and hamburgers or use as a topping for jacket potatoes.

Indonesian sauce   Serves 4–6

1 tablespoon salad oil
4 level tablespoons peanut
  butter
¼ pint tomato ketchup

3 tablespoons Worcestershire
  sauce
¼ teaspoon salt
garlic powder to taste

Heat the oil gently in a pan and add the peanut butter. Continue heating, gently, stirring occasionally until the peanut butter begins to thicken and darkens slightly. Immediately remove from the heat and stir in the tomato ketchup and Worcestershire sauce. Season to taste with garlic powder and salt. Leave for 2 hours before using. Reheat gently, and add a little water if the sauce is too thick. Serve with barbecued chicken and steaks; it can also be used to baste chicken.

Flavoured butters

Flavoured butter is a useful standby for the cook who has to prepare a meal quickly and wishes to allow his guests to select their own seasoning. The seasoned butters described below can be made up a few days before a barbecue party although it is not advisable to keep the butter more than a week after the seasoning has been added.

Seasoned butter can be added to a variety of foods including green vegetables, lamb chops, fish, chicken pieces, and some varieties also make a tasty sandwich spread.

Garlic butter

Cream ¼ lb butter or margarine with 2–3 finely minced cloves of garlic (not more than 1 teaspoon of minced garlic) and 1½ tablespoons of minced parsley. Cover and place in a refrigerator until required.

Garlic butter can be spread on seafood, grilled lamb chops, beef steaks, hot French bread or boiled new potatoes.

Lemon butter

Cream ¼ lb softened butter or margarine with 2 tablespoons lemon juice and 1 teaspoon of finely grated lemon peel.

Lemon butter can be spread over seafood, poultry or vegetables. Melt before using as a basting sauce.

Herb butter

Cream ¼ lb softened butter or margarine with ½ teaspoon tarragon or rosemary, 1 tablespoon finely chopped chives, ¾ tablespoon minced parsley, ⅛–¼ teaspoon of salt and a pinch of pepper. Cover and keep in a refrigerator until required.

Herb butter can be used with cooked vegetables, poultry, seafood and poached eggs. Try it as a sandwich spread.

Shallot butter

Lightly sauté 2 tablespoons chopped shallots in 1½ tablespoons of butter. The shallots should be soft enough to blend with other ingredients after about 5 minutes. Combine the shallots and ½ teaspoon of lemon juice with ¼ lb butter or margarine. Serve on seafood, cooked vegetables and chops, or use to baste chicken pieces.

Danish-blue butter

Combine ¼ lb butter or margarine with ¼ lb of Danish-blue cheese (crumbled), ¼ teaspoon paprika, and 2 tablespoons of double cream. Beat until light and fluffy. Cover and keep in a refrigerator until required.

Cheese butter is excellent when melted on steaks or hamburgers. It can also be used as a filling for baked potatoes and makes an appetizing sandwich spread.

Anchovy butter

Cream ¼ lb softened butter or margarine with 1½ tablespoons of anchovy paste and ¼ teaspoon of lemon juice. Anchovy butter is particularly suitable for spreading on grilled fish steaks or serving with most seafoods.

Chef's butter

Combine $\frac{1}{4}$ lb butter or margarine, 2 teaspoons minced parsley, $\frac{1}{4}$ teaspoon salt, 2 teaspoons lemon juice, $\frac{1}{4}$ teaspoon thyme and a pinch of pepper. Beat until light and fluffy. Cover and keep in a refrigerator until required.

Chef's butter is good for seasoning cooked vegetables and sautéed fish, or as a baste for grilled or roasted chicken.

Tarragon butter

Cream $\frac{1}{4}$ lb softened butter until light and fluffy. Blend in $\frac{1}{2}$ teaspoon grated lemon peel, 2 teaspoons lemon juice, 1 tablespoon finely chopped parsley, $\frac{1}{4}$ teaspoon salt and $\frac{1}{4}$ teaspoon dried, crushed tarragon.

Cover and keep in a refrigerator until required.

Tarragon butter is excellent for seasoning grilled steaks.

13   Vegetables, fruit and extras

Although the word barbecue evokes images of steaks sizzling on the grill or chickens slowly turning on the spit, the barbecue can cope with a far wider range of food than meat and fish. Most vegetables and fruit can be cooked directly on the barbecue grill, and others can be wrapped in foil and put on the grill or amongst hot coals to cook in their own, or added, juices. Vegetables and fruit are often part of shish-kebab recipes and hints on how to skewer-cook vegetables and fruit are given in Chapter 11.

When cooking unwrapped vegetables and fruit over a charcoal fire, it will be necessary to baste them frequently.

Vegetable kebabs   Serves 6

6 small potatoes	6 small tomatoes
6 small onions	2 oz melted butter
12 medium-size mushrooms	$\frac{1}{2}$ teaspoon garlic salt
2 green peppers	$\frac{1}{4}$ teaspoon black pepper

Peel potatoes and onions and cook, separately, in boiling salted water until they are barely tender. Remove stems from the mushrooms and wash the caps. Remove the seeds from the peppers and cut the peppers into twelve pieces. Drain the onions and potatoes and alternate on six skewers with the pieces of pepper and mushroom caps. Blend the melted butter, salt and pepper together, and brush the kebabs generously with the mixture. Cook with the grill set about 4–5 inches above hot coals. After 5 minutes add a tomato to each skewer, turn kebabs over and brush with more of the mixture. Continue cooking for another 5 minutes.

Stuffed peppers   Serves 6

6 large green peppers
4 oz Cheddar cheese
1¼ lb cooked haricot beans
tomato chili sauce (p. 136)

oregano
pinch garlic salt
freshly ground black pepper

Slice the tops from the peppers, remove the seeds and rinse well. Grate the cheese and put approximately 1 oz to one side. Stir the remainder of the cheese into the beans, stir in half the tomato sauce, and lightly season with oregano, garlic salt and pepper. Fill the peppers with the bean mixture and top each each pepper with a tablespoon of tomato sauce.

Wrap each pepper securely in a doubled piece of aluminium foil and grill over hot coals for 30–40 minutes, turning occasionally. Just before serving, open the foil packages and sprinkle cheese over top of each pepper.

Onions

Peel whole onions and cut into the stem end. Season with salt, pepper and a knob of butter. Wrap them individually in a double thickness of aluminium foil and place directly amongst hot coals. Medium-size onions should take approximately 30 minutes to become tender. Turn two or three times during cooking and test for doneness by piercing the onion, through the foil, with a long pointed skewer. Large onions should be cut into $\frac{1}{2}$-inch-thick slices and cooked in the manner described above.

Carrots

Select small, young carrots and scrub clean. Parboil until almost tender, remove from water and drain. Dip carrots in softened butter and barbecue over medium coals for approximately 5 minutes. Turn frequently and baste with melted butter.

Courgettes   Serves 4

4 medium-sized courgettes	salt
$\frac{1}{2}$ teaspoon oregano	freshly ground black pepper
4 tomatoes	3 oz butter or margarine

Parboil the courgettes for approximately 4 minutes in salted water to which the oregano has been added. Remove and slice each courgette into quarters. Place individual portions on a sheet of heavy-duty aluminium foil. Add chopped tomatoes, salt, freshly ground black pepper and a pat of butter or margarine. Wrap the foil securely around the food and barbecue over medium coals for approximately 15 minutes turning once.

Tomatoes with herbs   Serves 6

3 large tomatoes	$1\frac{1}{2}$ tablespoons chopped parsley
salt	
freshly ground black pepper	1 clove garlic, crushed
6 teaspoons butter, softened	$\frac{1}{2}$ teaspoon crushed tarragon
$1\frac{1}{2}$ tablespoons chopped spring onion	1 teaspoon dried oregano

Slice each tomato in half. Sprinkle each half with salt and pepper and top with one teaspoon of butter. Combine the remaining ingredients and sprinkle over tomatoes. Place tomatoes, cut surface up, in a foil pie-dish and cover tightly with a sheet of aluminium foil. Barbecue over medium coals for approximately 20 minutes, or until tender.

Grilled mushrooms in foil   Serves 4

1 lb mushrooms
3 tablespoons butter or
  margarine
salt

freshly ground black pepper
2 tablespoons dry sherry
  (optional)

Wash and cut mushroom stalks flush with caps. Place the mushrooms on a piece of doubled heavy-duty aluminium foil. Dot them with butter and sprinkle sparingly with salt and pepper, and add sherry if you are using it. Wrap the edges securely and grill over hot coals for approximately 15–20 minutes, turning the package occasionally.

Potatoes

Select medium-size, evenly shaped, potatoes that are suitable for jacket-baking, e.g. King Edward, Golden Wonder, Maris Piper or Pentland Ivory. Scrub well in cold water and pat dry with paper towel. Prick the skin with a knife point in several places and rub well with soft butter or margarine. After sprinkling with salt, wrap each potato tightly in heavy-duty foil (dull side out). Place the potatoes among the hot coals and bake for 40–50 minutes, turning every 4–5 minutes. Potatoes are done if they feel soft inside when gently pressed (with gloved hand or tongs). When soft cut through the foil, slice the potato part way through and pinch open. Fluff the potato with a fork and season to taste with butter or margarine, salt and freshly ground black pepper. Garnish with a sprig of parsley.

Sour cream, mixed with finely chopped chives, may be used in place of butter.

NOTE: By using parboiled potatoes the cooking time will be considerably reduced.

Potatoes with onion

Parboil medium-sized potatoes, remove the skins and cut each potato into four thick slices.

Onion can be added in either of the following ways:

1. Place onion slices, approximately $\frac{1}{8}$ inch thick, between the potato sections and re-assemble potato.
2. Blend 3 oz of softened butter with 6 oz finely chopped onion, spread on the potato sections and re-assemble the potato.

Place each potato on a square of heavy-duty foil, top with a knob of butter and wrap the foil tightly around the potato in order to keep the sections close together. Place the potatoes among the hot coals and bake for approximately 30 minutes or, if using sliced onions, for about 40 minutes until the onion is tender.

NOTE. Foil-wrapped potatoes can be baked on barbecue grills, bearing in mind that this method of cooking will take several minutes longer than cooking potatoes directly on hot coals.

Corn on the cob 1

Select tender, fresh sweetcorn in the husks, allowing one corn cob for each guest. Corn can be barbecued in various ways.

Remove corn husks and silk, then rinse well in salted iced

water. Place each ear on a sheet of heavy-duty aluminium foil and brush on ½ oz of softened butter. Sprinkling one table-spoon of water over the ear of corn, wrap securely and place in the barbecue coals for 15–20 minutes, turning several times.

Allow approximately twice as long when cooking corn on the barbecue grill.

Corn on the cob 2

Remove the large outer corn husk, turn back the inner husks and remove the silk. Rinse well in salted iced water, brush the corn generously with garlic butter (see p. 138). Replace husks over ear and hold them into place with fine wire. (Position wire near each end and in centre). Roast on the barbecue grill over hot coals for 15–20 minutes, turning every 5 minutes. Before serving cut the wire and remove the husks (gloves will be needed for this operation).

Corn on the cob 3

Remove corn husks and silk. Remove the rind from a rasher of fat bacon, wrap the bacon around the corn and secure with cocktail sticks. Barbecue over hot coals for approximately 15–20 minutes, turning frequently, or until the bacon is crisp and the uncovered areas of corn are golden brown.

Fruit kebabs

Make up individual skewers by threading any combination of the following fruits: pineapple chunks, a wedge of eating apple, a ½-inch-thick half-slice of orange (with the peel on), a section of banana about 1½ inches long, half an apricot, a large black grape. Before grilling brush the fruit with melted butter, and baste frequently during cooking. An excellent baste for fruit kebabs is ginger-flavoured butter; this is made by stirring one teaspoon of ground ginger and one tablespoon of sugar into $\frac{1}{4}$ lb of melted butter.

Apples

Wash and dry apple and cut (unpeeled) into $\frac{1}{2}$-inch-thick slices. Dip slices in melted butter and grill on both sides until tender. During the last few minutes of cooking, sprinkle slices with cinnamon and sugar.

Oranges

Wash and dry orange and cut into $\frac{3}{4}$-inch-thick slices. Dip slices in melted butter and lightly dust with flour. Barbecue both sides until orange is warmed through.

Spiced apples   Serves 6

6 medium-sized cooking apples
4 oz brown sugar
2 teaspoons ground cinnamon
1$\frac{1}{2}$ oz finely chopped walnuts
1$\frac{1}{2}$ oz finely chopped raisins
6 teaspoons butter or margarine
whipped cream or vanilla ice-cream for serving

Wash and core the apples. Place each on a piece of doubled aluminium foil. Combine brown sugar, cinnamon, walnuts and raisins, and fill the centres of the apples with the mixture. Top each apple with a teaspoon of butter and wrap the edges of foil securely. Barbecue on the grill, over medium coals, for approximately 40–50 minutes or for 25–30 minutes directly on the coals. The apples are cooked when soft.

Serve topped with whipped cream or vanilla ice-cream.

Spiced bananas Individual serving

1 firm banana	pinch of cinnamon
lemon juice	1 teaspoon butter or
1 tablespoon brown sugar	margarine

Peel the banana and place on a double thickness of aluminium foil. Brush generously with lemon juice. Sprinkle brown sugar evenly over the banana and dust with ground cinnamon. Dot with butter and wrap edges of foil securely. Barbecue on the grill, over medium coals, for approximately 8 minutes or directly on the coals for approximately 5 minutes.

Chocolate banana split Individual serving

1 firm banana	3 marshmallows (cut into
1 oz dark chocolate (cut into	quarters)
small chips)	

Peel the banana and cut out a wedge along its length, approximately $\frac{1}{2}$-inch wide and $\frac{1}{2}$-inch deep. Fill the cavity in the banana with chocolate chips and top with the marshmallow pieces. Press the banana wedge back into place and lay the banana on a double thickness of aluminium foil. Wrap edges of foil securely and barbecue on the grill, over hot coals, for approximately 10 minutes – or until the chocolate and marshmallow melts and the banana is tender.

Spiced peaches Serves 4

4 peaches, skinned, halved	1 tablespoon Worcestershire
and stones removed	sauce
2 oz soft brown sugar	

Place the sugar and Worcestershire sauce in pan and heat very gently until the sugar has dissolved. Spoon this mixture over the peaches and leave for 2–3 hours, turning the peaches occasionally. Drain and place the peaches on the barbecue grill over medium coals, until browned.

Spiced peaches go well with barbecued bacon or ham.

Grilled peaches   Serves 6

12 peach halves (canned or fresh)

4 oz butter or margarine

3 tablespoons sweet sherry or rum

For each serving place two peach halves, cut side down, on a double thickness of aluminium foil (turn edges of foil up slightly). Brush softened butter over the peach halves and barbecue over hot coals for approximately 5 minutes. Mix the sherry or rum into the remaining butter, turn the warmed peaches over and spoon the flavoured butter into the cavities. Make sure the edges of the foil are turned up securely and barbecue for approximately 8–10 minutes.

Serve topped with whipped cream, or ice-cream, and garnish with a few chopped almonds.

Barbados oranges   Individual serving

1 orange (preferably seedless)

1 tablespoon brown sugar

pinch of cinnamon

1 tablespoon rum

1 teaspoon butter or margarine

Peel the orange (take out pips if necessary), and separate into segments. Place them on a double thickness of aluminium foil. Sprinkle with brown sugar and add the cinnamon and rum. Dot the segments with butter and wrap the edges of the foil securely. Barbecue on the grill, over medium coals, for approximately 15–20 minutes or directly on the coals for approximately 10–15 minutes.

Serve topped with whipped cream or ice-cream.

Honey pineapple   Serves 8

1 medium-sized fresh pineapple	8 tablespoons honey

Remove the top from the pineapple and cut into eight lengthwise wedges. Remove the centre core. Place each wedge on a double thickness of aluminium foil and spread a tablespoonful of honey over the fruit. Allow to stand for 40–50 minutes. Wrap edges of foil securely and barbecue on the grill, over medium coals, for approximately 20 minutes or directly on the coals for approximately 15 minutes. Turn the foil packages once during cooking.

These pineapple wedges are an excellent garnish for pork chops, spareribs or ham.

Grilled grapefruit   Serves 6

3 grapefruit	3 tablespoons honey or
3 tablespoons sweet sherry (optional)	brown sugar
	6 maraschino cherries

Cut the grapefruit in half, cutting loose the segments and removing pips. Place each half on a double thickness of aluminium foil and spoon about $\frac{1}{2}$ tablespoon of honey and $\frac{1}{2}$ tablespoon of sherry over it. Put a cherry in the centre of each half and wrap the edges of the foil securely. Cook on the grill over medium coals, cut side up, for approximately 15 minutes.

Barbecued French bread   Serves 6–8

Slice a loaf of French bread in half lengthwise. Spread with one of the seasoned butters given in Chapter 12. Wrap each half in heavy-duty aluminium foil, dull side out, and barbecue on the grill set 4–5 inches above medium coals. Heat for approximately 10 minutes, turning two or three times. During the last 3–4 minutes of cooking open the foil to allow the charcoal flavour to permeate the bread.

For a change, sprinkle grated Parmesan cheese on the bread and add a pinch of paprika before serving.

Hot garlic bread   Serves 6–8

1 small white loaf (unsliced)   4 oz garlic butter (recipe
  or a French stick   (p. 138)
    poppy seeds (optional)

Cut the small loaf in half lengthwise, almost through to the bottom, and then crosswise at one inch intervals. A French loaf will only need to be cut crosswise. Place it on a sheet of heavy-duty aluminium foil and brush all cut and outside surfaces of the bread with melted garlic butter. The top and sides of loaf may be sprinkled with poppy seeds. Wrap the foil securely around the loaf and heat over medium coals for approximately 12 minutes, turning once.

Serve hot after cutting through the bottom of the loaf to free the segments.

Cheese and herb rolls   Serves 8

8 rolls   1 tablespoon finely chopped
6 oz butter, softened   onion

4 oz blue cheese or grated
  Cheddar cheese
1 teaspoon crushed rosemary

1½ tablespoons chopped
  parsley
1 teaspoon dried basil

Slice the rolls in half. Combine the remaining ingredients and spread the mixture on the cut sides of each roll. Place the halves together and wrap securely in pieces of aluminium foil. Place on the grill and barbecue, over medium coals, for approximately 15 minutes or until hot.

Bacon and onion rolls   Serves 8

8 crusty rolls
4 rashers bacon (streaky or
  short back)

3 oz butter, softened
1 medium-size onion, finely
  chopped

Cut the rind off the bacon, grill until crisp and finely chop. Combine butter, bacon pieces and the chopped onion. Split the rolls and spread the mixture on the cut side of each half. Place halves together again, wrap securely in pieces of aluminium foil and barbecue over medium coals for approximately 15 minutes, turning several times.

Hot onion bread

2 12-inch Vienna sticks
6 oz butter

1 level teaspoon onion
  powder

Cream together butter and onion powder. Make five cuts along each loaf to within ½ inch of the bottom. Spread the mixture between the cuts. Wrap the loaves in aluminium foil and cook on the grill, above medium coals, for about 15 minutes.

To serve, finish cutting between slices.

Cider cup   Serves 12

¼ bottle lemon squash
¼ bottle orange squash
2 pints of cider
½ pint of fruit juice

grated rind of one lemon
½ glass sherry
sprigs of crushed mint
ice cubes

Place ice cubes in a large jug, add remaining ingredients and mix well. Allow to stand for about an hour before serving.

Hot spiced fruit punch   Serves 6

¼ pint orange squash
¼ pint white wine
½ pint port
1½ tablespoons castor sugar

1 small stick of cinnamon
grated rind of a lemon
pinch of ground ginger

Place all the ingredients in a saucepan and bring to the boil. Flame the punch, then allow it to burn out. Strain the liquid and retain in a vacuum flask until required.

Hock cup   Serves 14

2 bottles of hock, or riesling
4 fl. oz brandy
½ pint soda water
1½ fl. oz orange curaçao
½ teaspoon Angostura bitters

3–4 sprigs of mint or borage
    (bruised)
small quantity of thinly
    sliced orange, strawberries,
    apple, pineapple, etc.
a few ice cubes

Place all the ingredients, except the ice cubes, in a large jug about an hour or so before serving. Mix well and add ice immediately prior to serving.

Mulled red wine   Serves 4–6

1 bottle of red wine
juice of 2 oranges
juice of 1 lemon
1 tablespoon of brandy

4 oz sugar lumps
1 cinnamon stick
2 cloves
lemon slices (for serving)

Place the wine and sugar in a saucepan and stir over a gentle heat until the sugar has dissolved. Add the remaining ingredients and bring slowly to simmering point, stirring continuously. Strain the wine into a pre-warmed jug and warm the glasses you intend to serve it in. Top each glass with a slice of lemon.

Standard weights and measures

Liquid measures

British

1 quart	= 2 pints	= 40 fl. oz
1 pint	= 4 gills	= 20 fl. oz
½ pint	= 2 gills	
	or one cup	= 10 fl. oz
¼ pint	= 8 tablespoons	= 5 fl. oz
	1 tablespoon	= just over ½ fl. oz
	1 dessertspoon	= ⅓ fl. oz
	1 teaspoon	= ⅙ fl. oz

Metric

1 litre = 10 decilitres (dl) = 100 centilitres (cl) = 1,000 millilitres (ml)

American

1 quart	= 2 pints	= 32 fl. oz
1 pint	= 2 cups	= 16 fl. oz
	1 cup	= 8 fl. oz
	1 tablespoon	= ⅓ fl. oz
	1 teaspoon	= ⅙ fl. oz

Approx. equivalents

British	Metric	American
1 quart	1·1 litre	2½ pints
1 pint	6 dl	1¼ pints
½ pint	3 dl	10 fl. oz (1¼ cups)
¼ pint (1 gill)	1·5 dl	5 fl. oz
1 tablespoon	15 ml	1½ tablespoons
1 dessertspoon	10 ml	1 tablespoon
1 teaspoon	5 ml	$\frac{1}{6}$ fl. oz

Metric	British and American
1 litre	35 fl. oz
½ litre (5 dl)	18 fl. oz
¼ litre (2·5 dl)	9 fl. oz
1 dl	3½ fl. oz

American	British	Metric
1 quart	1½ pints + 3 tbs (32 fl. oz)	9·5 dl
1 pint	¾ pint + 2 tbs (16 fl. oz)	4·7 dl
1 cup	½ pint — 3 tbs (8 fl. oz)	2·4 dl

Solid measures

Approx. equivalents

British	Metric	Metric	British
1 lb (16 oz)	450 g	1 kg (1,000 g)	2 lb 3 oz
½ lb (8 oz)	225 g	½ kg (500 g)	1 lb 2 oz
¼ lb (4 oz)	110 g	¼ kg (250 g)	9 oz
1 oz	25 g	100 g	3½ oz

All spoon measurements in this book indicate level spoonfuls.

Index to Recipes